Wilderness Wanderings

...devotions from the desert

Great are the works of the Lord;
they are pondered by all who delight in them.

Psalm 111:2

Marti Evans

Partnership
Publications

Partnership Publications
www.h2hp.com

Wilderness Wanderings…devotions from the desert
by Marti Evans

© 2018 by Marti Evans

Published by
Partnership Publications
A Division of House To House Publications
11 Toll Gate Road, Lititz, PA, USA
Tele: 717.627.1996

www.h2hp.com

ISBN-13: 978-0-9962924-9-8
ISBN-10: 0-9962924-9-7

Note: Some names have been changed.

Endorsements

"A wise man once said, 'God calls us to the wilderness in order to make us His daughters and sons.' Until we learn this lesson, all our sorrows will only be wasted. Marti realized her daughterhood in a wilderness she marvelously articulates in the devotions in this book. In it, she invites you and me to wander through her wilderness and discover the loving kindness of the Father who never leaves us or forsakes us."

— *Michael Card, Bible scholar, songwriter, author*

"Marti, in her journaling, allows us to look over her shoulder to see events in her life up front and close. Then she transparently invites us into her heart to experience her walk with the Lord, step by step, into the promised land. Authenticity and reverence portray her growing faith—opening doors for us to ponder our own journey."

— *Keith E. Yoder, Ed. D., author, founder of Teaching the Word Ministries*

"Thanks to Marti for being brave enough to share the good, the bad, the ugly and the uglier during this particular season of life. Her faith filled perspectives have given me pause to reflect anew on God's promises kept and those yet to come. You will be blessed as you make this journey with Marti."

— *Rachel Kerr Schneider, author, founder of Spirited Prosperity*

Dedication

This book is dedicated to Jesus, who has become for me
every relationship that I needed to be healed from;
father, husband, brother and friend.

To my children; Brian, Lauren and Shannon, and their spouses
Amanda, Chris and Ryan and my grandchildren; Clay, Nolan, Reed,
Trevor, Dylan, Parker, Katelyn, Olive and Alison,
may you always know that Jesus is real.
I love you.

Acknowledgements

I am so very grateful for the people God brought into my life, at just the right time, to contribute to the completion of *Wilderness Wanderings...devotions from the desert.*

To the sweet ladies that helped to compose questions at the end of each section, taking this book from a devotional to a resource for a Bible study or discussion group, I am humbled by your input. Thank you Angie Diller, Heidi Fittery, Paula Horst, Brenda Kocher, Carol Kohr, Shari Spencer, Laurie Stone, Judy Walton and Lori Yaw.

Special thanks to those who lent me the use of their properties for secluded times to write: Kerry and Becky Ritts, the farmhouse in Sullivan County, PA, Brian and Amanda Evans, the beach house in Ocean City, MD, and Mark and Gail Spencer, the prayer cabin in Cortland, NY.

The beautiful interior photos were taken by my daughter at Shannon Fretz Photography. The front cover was captured by Susan Surman in the Judean Desert, just as we were about to board the bus to go to the next location on a tour of Israel.

Each of your gifts were an invaluable part of this book. You are dearly loved and I am deeply grateful.

Contents

Introduction

Nevertheless, as surely as I live and as surely as the glory of the Lord fills the whole earth, not one of the men who saw My glory and the miraculous signs I performed in Egypt and in the desert but who disobeyed Me and tested Me ten times – not one of them will ever see the land I promised on oath to their forefathers. Numbers 14:21-23

I was thrust into the desert, not unlike the children of the Israelites. There, not by their disobedience, but by their relatives' rebellion against God. And so it was with me. On February 23, 2002, my husband, the love of my life, announced that he was leaving me. Again. He had been home for fifteen months and all seemed well. As I look back at how God has worked, I see so clearly this was my entrance into the wilderness. Not spurred by my rebellion, but rather by my husband's. As I have stood with God for the healing of my family, I have experienced the consequences and the testing of that obedience.

I sought God's face, His direction and His presence. And He did not fail me. I praise Him for walking with me in the wilderness and meeting my every need.

One morning, I asked my daughter, Lauren, to take my journals and make three copies of them; one for her, one for Shannon and one for Brian, my precious children. I recalled to her the story of Elijah, noting that God spared him from the experience of death as He transported him to heaven in a whirlwind. I wondered if the Lord would do that for me as well, for the pain was so great. Without hesitation, my daughter said, "Okay." I was so blessed by that. No argument. No declaration that I should not talk that way. She understood the depth of my grief, for my children were experiencing it as well.

I wanted my children to know that God is real. Really real.

He is alive.

Here is some of what He has taught me about:

- His Presence
- His Provision
- His Protection
- His Power
- His Promises
- His Peace
- His Plans

He sustained me in the wilderness and brought me into His Promised Land.

His Presence

*The Lord replied, "My Presence will go with you,
and I will give you rest."*

Exodus 33:14

Who am I?

It was my birthday. I just could not go into the office and pretend that everything was okay, hear all the good wishes, when I knew that my life was spinning out of control. My husband had become more and more distant and the harder I tried to fix it, the worse things got. I didn't know what to do.

I headed up north to a favorite vacation spot. I sat at the beach by the lake. Just me, the Lord, my Bible and my journal. I wrote and wrote...all my feelings and fears spilled out. I cried. I was so afraid. To go home. To stay away. To face the future. I had no idea what was happening. I only knew that I was more frightened than I had ever been in my life.

After several hours I drove toward home, still crying, still praying, and still scared. I came to a stop light just a few miles from home. I will never forget it. I was driving my shiny red car with the sunroof open and the air conditioner on when the Lord spoke to me:

"You are a princess."

At first I was startled to so clearly hear His voice. Then He continued on...

"I love you. You know the thing about princesses is that they have a life that does not include worrying. They have plenty to eat, they live in the finest homes, they have lovely things to wear and they are so well taken care of. Royalty. You are royalty. You are my princess and I will take care of you."

Within two weeks my husband left me and moved out.

Then he returned.

Then he left again.

Through many dark days and nights, the Lord still speaks.

I am a daughter of the King. A princess.

Because you are sons, God sent the Spirit of His Son into our hearts, the Spirit who calls out, "Abba Father." So you are no longer a slave, but a son; and since you are a son, God has made you also an heir. Galatians 4:6-7

Psalm 23

I worked in my real estate profession all day Saturday...several appointments, then handled an Open House until 3:00. That's when my weekend starts. I headed home, trying to reach my husband on his cell phone. No answer. It wasn't until after 6:00 p.m. that he walked into the house. He sat me down at the dining room table and proceeded to pour devastation upon me. I had no idea. I just didn't.

We had been through counseling for six months and he had been home for fifteen months. As he confessed his actions to me, hope welled in me, for now we could get help.

"No. I am leaving you."

And he did. Right then, that very night.

I wasn't sure what to do. Shock describes it, but not really.

Lauren was at her job at the George Washington Tavern. Brian was stationed as an Air Force lieutenant in Florida. Shannon was away at college. Should I call them? What would I say? It was after midnight when Lauren arrived home. Where is Dad? And then I told her. How do you handle your 22-year-old daughter crumbling to the floor right in front of you? How do you comfort her when your own heart is breaking?

I made a valiant effort to sleep that night. I piled pillows on the side of the bed so I wouldn't feel so alone.

How many pillows does a husband make?

All night long, I wrestled. And all night long the words of the 23rd Psalm came into my mind and out of my mouth. I didn't really know the 23rd Psalm, had never memorized it, but there it was, over and over again.

"...the Lord is my Shepherd...I will not be in want...He guides me in paths of righteousness…even though I walk through the valley of the shadow of death… I will fear no evil…You anoint my head with oil…surely goodness and love will follow me all the days of my life…"

After a fitful sleep, the night was over. It was Sunday morning. How could I go to church? What would I say? How could I explain what had just happened when I didn't even understand it myself? Lauren suggested I go with her and her boyfriend to their church. That felt safe…I didn't know anyone there. I shared with Lauren how all through the night the 23rd Psalm just kept coming to me, even though I had never memorized it.

Arriving at their church, numb with despair, Lauren and I grabbed one another's hands as Pastor Bill announced a new sermon series… on the 23rd Psalm.

"The Lord is Marti's shepherd; she shall not be in want. He makes Marti lie down in green pastures; He leads Marti beside quiet waters, He restores Marti's soul. He guides Marti in paths of righteousness for His name's sake. Even though Marti walks through the valley of the shadow of death, Marti will fear no evil, for You are with Marti, Your rod and Your staff comfort Marti. You prepare a table before Marti in the presence of her enemies. You anoint Marti's head with oil; Marti's cup overflows. Surely goodness and love will follow Marti all the days of her life, and Marti will dwell in the house of the Lord forever."

He has me memorized.

Forever starts now.

Jesus on the Bench

I have to confess. I didn't always look in the right places for help. A friend recommended a woman she knew who held "healing" sessions in her home. She was kind. She promoted the healing of past wounds. She used unconventional methods.

One day, during a private session, she talked me through an imagery practice. I don't really think there is anything wrong with that, except that she didn't invite Jesus into her methods. New Age, I suppose you would call it. I was ignorant.

Until one particular day.

She had me close my eyes and think back to a favorite place of mine, where I had been happy and at peace. Next, she wanted me to imagine myself sitting on a bench in the sunshine. "Now, invite someone who has been important to you in your life to join you…like a parent, a friend, a mentor…someone who will guide you in life," she instructed. As I lay still with my eyes closed and saw myself at the farmhouse in the mountains that we used to own, Jesus came and sat down on the bench.

The counselor carried on, "Now put someone else on the bench, someone you feel will guide you through life, like a spouse, a friend, or even Buddha."

Jesus just sat there on my bench. He didn't move. He crossed His ankle over His knee, leaned against the bench, rested His arm along the back and smiled. Jesus wasn't moving off my bench.

I never went back to her for counsel, for I had the great Counselor, who promised never to leave me or forsake me. He was the only One I needed to invite into my life.

For this God is our God forever and ever; He will be our guide even to the end. Psalm 48:14

The T-shirt Story

How do you go through your days after you've been abandoned?How many times had I cried out to God and asked Him this question: "What do you require of me?" How many times had I written that very question in my journal? I was following God the best I knew how, searching my heart, confessing my own sin, begging Him to show me how to go on…

Sometimes, it is really hard to stay home and be reminded that indeed you are alone.

So, sometimes you just go shopping.

Lauren and I headed down to Park City Mall, a nearby shopping center. It was a cold, mid-October evening. As we entered the mall, there was an Arby's restaurant. Lauren asked if I had eaten yet today. I shook my head; she marched us right in there and ordered a sandwich and fries. Sitting in the booth, my daughter urged me to eat just one more bite (I wondered when the roles reversed and the daughter became the mom and the mom became the daughter). I looked up to see a man walking past our booth. I couldn't help but notice he was wearing shorts and a t-shirt on this chilly night. There was writing on the shirt, but I couldn't read it. But I could make out that it said at the bottom *Micah 6:8*. "Micah 6:8," I said out loud. "I should look that up."

Now granted, we were at the mall. There were several bookstores that I could have gone to, grabbed a Bible and found out what *Micah 6:8* says.

But, I confess I just simply forgot about it.

The next morning, I opened up a devotional that automatically comes into my e-mail account. At the top, it said this:

And what does the Lord require of you? To act justly and to love mercy and to walk humbly with your God. Micah 6:8.

He answers my questions. Sometimes in the most unlikely places, like on the back of a t-shirt, but He answers nonetheless.

In my grief, in my suffering, He is there, still speaking, still instructing, still loving. He loved me enough to answer me again, when I couldn't hear Him the first time.

Act justly.
Love mercy.
Walk humbly before my God.

That is what He requires of me.

Empty Closet, Empty Tomb

It was Good Friday and the office was closed.

I was really sick; achy, stuffy, feverish, lying on the couch because I did not even have enough energy to get a shower.

There was a knock at the door.

Surprise…there was my spouse, unexpectedly coming to remove the rest of his things from our home. Not a welcome sight and me, oh so unsightly. It was not the way I would have arranged it had I been in control.

I watched in intense sorrow as he moved his belongings out. Oh, how I had prayed this day would never come. Surely, God could intervene even now.

He wanted to tell me again that he was divorcing me whether I wanted it or not. And the whole thing would be smoother if I just agreed. I had no energy to argue and quietly stated again that I did not want a divorce.

When he was finished removing his things, he left. I wandered into the bedroom to assess the damage and entered the walk-in closet to see his whole side of the closet now empty. Somehow, I had taken security in those clothes hanging there.

I huddled in a ball on the floor, weeping. I sensed the still, small voice of my Lord speak to me.

"Marti, this empty closet is just like the empty tomb. Jesus had to die before He could rise again. And I say to you: your marriage has to die, so I can bring you new life. I made you a promise and I keep My promises."

Hope renewed.

It's Friday, but Sunday is coming.

The Mailbox Verse

It is a fearful thing to dread bad news.

I pick up my mail at the local post office. There's no home delivery in the small village where I live.

One day while reading the Bible, this verse struck me:

He will have no fear of bad news; his heart is steadfast, trusting in the Lord. Psalm 112:7

It literally became my mantra as I drove into the post office parking lot, took a deep breath, entered the building and inserted the key into the box, all the while declaring that I would not be afraid. Bad news could not hurt me as long as I kept my eyes on Jesus.

The bad news did come. Over and over again.

Papers.

Lots of papers.

Threats. Sign or else it will cost lots of money.

Sign saying your marriage is "irreconcilable."

How can that be?

What is irreconcilable with God?

Absolutely nothing, for Jesus Himself is the Reconciler.

My sight remained on Him and He brought me through.

Therefore, if anyone is in Christ, he is a new creation; the old has gone, the new has come! All this is from God, who reconciled us to Himself through Christ and gave us the ministry of reconciliation: that God was reconciling the world to Himself in Christ, not counting men's sins against them. And He has committed to us the message of reconciliation. 2 Corinthians 5:17-19

In the Garden

My brother Stephen and his wife, Amy, surprised me with a basket full of "flip-flop" things for my summer birthday – plaques and magnets, a pair of pink and yellow flowered flip flops and lots more.

One day, my four year old grandson, Clay, found the basket in the closet and was enjoying looking through all the treasures, when he came across ceramic flip-flops to be used as garden stones. We headed out to the backyard with them and as Clay and I were deciding where to put them, I placed them in the ground as if they were taking a step. I joked with Clay that it looks like someone is walking in Grandma's garden.

In his sweet, innocent voice, he said, "Maybe it is God!"

It reminded me of the chorus of the old hymn that is precious to our family. I taught Clay the words: "And He walks with me. And He talks with me. And He tells me I am His own. And the joy we share as we tarry there, none other has ever known."

The story goes like this. When Clay's grandfather was a little younger than Clay, about three years old, he was with his family in church and this hymn had just been sung. He looked up at his mother and asked, "Who's Andy?"

Precious.

Just precious.

God is walking in my garden and I experienced inexpressible joy as Clay and I met Him there.

He will teach us His ways, so that we may walk in His paths. Isaiah 2:3

Hope

The sharp downturn in the economy eventually resulted in the closing of my real estate office. Having spent six months looking for a new opportunity, I was grateful for the part-time position in a chiropractor's office. I was on a 40-minute lunch break, taking advantage of the warm and windy spring day to walk around the path through the adjoining community. In the center was a playground.

I was chatting with the Lord as I walked, wondering again how all this could possibly work. How was I going to survive on the limited hours I was working? How much longer until I would see healing in my family? How could I not succumb to the persistent feelings of loneliness and discouragement? I declared I was trusting Him, yet could not "see" how His plan was going to unfold. So, I asked Him if He could just give me new hope today.

On the second trip through the neighborhood, I had an urge to stop and swing for a bit at the playground. A little girl waved to me from the sliding board. She was with her daddy. She took his hand and led him over to the swing next to me. With such sweet words, she told me that she was three years old, but almost three-and-a-half. I showed her how to pump her legs so we could reach the sky together.

And we did. I felt free and like a little girl myself.

Soon, it was time for me to get back to the office. Before I left, she asked my name.

"My name is Marti, but my grandkids call me Grandma MJ. What is your name?"

"My name is Hope."

And so it was that at the very moment I needed it, He sent me "new" Hope.

Hope.

On a swing.

The Lord is good to those whose hope is in Him, to the one who seeks Him; it is good to wait quietly for the salvation of the Lord. Lamentations 3:25-26

Be

The voices were clamoring.

Loudly.

What will you do? This is what you should do. Could you do this? Did you try to do this? You have to do something.

Do! Do! Do!

The Voice is quietly whispering.

Be. Just be.

Be. Be. Be.

Be...in My presence.
Be...quiet.
Be...still.
Be...content.
Be...fearless.
Be...empty.
Be...filled.
Be...loved by Me.

Be-loved daughter.

One. Voice. Is. All. I. Need. To. Hear.

Speak, Lord, for Your servant is listening. 1 Samuel 3:9

Alive Again

Trail walking with Jesus is what I do in the early morning hour, sometimes before the fullness of the day's light has burst forth. On this particular morning, on the way back to the house, I was startled to see the crepe myrtle bush near the edge of the fence at the bottom of the yard was in bloom. A gift from my "forever friends" in memory of my mother's life had appeared to be dead. My landscaper son-in-law had even declared it to be so. The harsh winter had taken its toll.

This was actually its second death. It was transplanted when I moved to the historic stone house the year before. It seemed to not fare the move too well, but then a late "surprise" bloom appeared.

I snapped a photo and went inside for some coffee and conversation with Jesus. I opened the Word to read through *John 11* for that evening's Bible study.

Lazarus had been dead for four days, smelling of rotten flesh, when Jesus finally arrived. He actually could have come earlier, but purposely delayed. Mary and Martha, the sisters of Lazarus, let Jesus know He was late and if only He had hurried, their brother would not have died. To which Jesus replied:

Your brother will rise again. John 11:23

Jesus came to the tomb and commanded that the stone be rolled away. Martha protested that Lazarus' body was already decaying. Jesus said to her:

Did I not tell you that if you believed, you would see the glory of God? John 11:40

So, they removed the stone. Jesus thanked His Father that He heard Him and that this large crowd that had gathered to comfort Martha and Mary will now believe in Him because of the miracle they were about to witness.

Jesus shouted in a loud voice, "Lazarus, come out!" John 11:43

And he did.

The once-dead Lazarus was alive again.

The twice-dead crepe myrtle was alive again.

I pondered all this as I read and sipped...Jesus has the final word. Jesus, the Creator, the Resurrection and the Life, the Alpha and the Omega, the Word that became flesh. He has the final word. He is the final Word.

What appears dead in my life: hopes, dreams, desires, relationships, may only be sleeping. Jesus may be delayed, but He is never late. Jesus said to me:

Did I not tell you that if you believed, you would see the glory of God? John 11:40

I believe.

Pause to Ponder

- What benefits are yours as God's child? Ask Him to wondrously show Himself to you and who you are in Him.

- Share an example of a difficult time when you focused on God instead of the problem.

- God cares for His children. Has there been an instance when He has pursued you? How did He do that and what was the result?

- How does knowing He is with you change your response to difficult circumstances? Reflect on *Deuteronomy 31:6*.

- What are you dreading today? What can you do to keep your eyes on God?

- List some ways you can find joy during trials. Is there a Scripture that you turn to during these times?

- When was the last time you intentionally took time away to be still and ask God to reveal Himself to you?

- What examples can you think of from your own life when God brought back to life what you thought was dead?

His Provision

He provides food for those who fear Him;
He remembers His covenant forever.

Psalm 111:5

The Tithe

"What are we going to do, Lord?"

That was my question as I walked along the trail, talking out loud to Him. His answer took me by surprise.

"You are going to tithe." Seriously?

Many years ago we faithfully tithed, as we were challenged at a service one day to do so. When my husband walked away from the Lord, he declared that we would no longer give to the church. I felt I needed to honor him in that decision. We did continue to give to a few local para-church ministries that we had been involved with, but discontinued giving 10 percent off the top of our income.

Now I was crying out to the Lord. My husband had just left with three-quarters of our income. The answer the Lord gave me made absolutely no sense. I have since learned that those "no sense" answers are most often from Him.

I did argue with Him about the sensibility of these instructions, but to no avail. I wanted to be in obedience. I desired His will in my life more than even life itself.

So, I obeyed.

From that day on, anything that came into my home, I set aside 10 percent for God's work. And He never failed me, for His Word is true:

"Bring the whole tithe into the storehouse, that there may be food in My house. Test Me in this," says the Lord Almighty, "and see if I will not open the floodgates of heaven and pour out so much blessing that you will not have room enough for it." Malachi 3:10

I brought the tithe.

He sent the blessings.

Rent the Tent

Shannon and Ryan were married at the Cornwall Church on Friday evening and the reception was held in my beautiful back yard, just a few blocks from the church.

I really had no idea how I was going to pay for the weddings.

Yes. Weddings.

Shannon and Ryan on May 30th and Lauren and Chris on August 16th.

Little did I know at the time, there was another one to come…Brian and Amanda on January 30th of the next year.

Three weddings in nine months!

God said He would provide…and He did.

Chris was the high school baseball coach and each year hosted an end-of-the-year picnic for the parents and the players. Well, this year, they had yet to secure a location. A week or so before the wedding, he asked me if they could have it in my backyard, since we would already have the tent up and the rental company would not be coming to remove it until Monday. The picnic was scheduled for Saturday, so I gladly agreed to help him out. Much to my surprise, a few days before the wedding, Chris brought me a check from the Parents Club to cover their portion of the tent rental!

WOW…who could have planned that?

Only He who knows what I need before I even ask Him.

If you then, though you are evil, know how to give good gifts to your children, how much more will your Father in heaven give good gifts to those who ask Him! Matthew 7:11

Free Fall

I let go.

Again.

But this time, it felt different.

I had been dangling by a thread, trying to figure out what to do… watching the money slip away…seeing no income in sight…begging for insight…longing for assurance. And now my resources are gone.

It isn't quite the same as trusting God when I had money in my savings account.

I was an hour into my walk on the Rails to Trails, hiding my tears behind my sunglasses, when I identified the feeling.

Afraid, yet filled with joy.

The story of the women going to the tomb to find Jesus came to my mind, and I thought I'd look it up when I got home.

It really was a beautiful day for a *free fall*.

Crystal blue, cloudless sky.

Reminded me of the surprise para-sailing adventure with Brian and Amanda, on the trip they paid for me to join them in Hawaii. The view from six hundred feet was spectacular! I was a bit fearful on the way down (on the way up, too). I didn't really want to land in the water. I could hear Brian, on the boat with Trevor and Parker, telling the man guiding us back in: "Please don't put my Mom in the water." And he didn't. I was so grateful. Amanda and I were gently guided onto the boat deck.

Three days after His crucifixion, on the first day of the week, some women went to the tomb to anoint Jesus' body with spices. But His body wasn't there. Instead they ran into two men in gleaming, white clothes who told them that Jesus wasn't there because He had risen from the dead, just as He told them He would.

So the women hurried away from the tomb, afraid, yet filled with joy. Matthew 28:8

I just love what happened next…

Suddenly Jesus met them. Matthew 28:9

As I let go and trust God completely to be my provider, as He has promised, I don't expect to land in the water and sink to the bottom of the ocean.

I expect to land on solid ground.

I expect Jesus to suddenly meet me.

Am I afraid?

I sure am.

Afraid.

…yet, filled with joy.

The Lights are on, But...

How does that saying go?

The lights are on, but no one is home.

My electric bill comes to me automatically by e-mail. It stated that I had a $125 credit.

Well, how could that be?

Unbeknownst to me, a friend had sent a payment directly to the electric company on my behalf.

With amazement and gratitude, I recalled the words of Scripture:

...for your Father knows what you need before you ask Him. Matthew 6:8

These words rang true. Before I had even been issued a bill for the month's electric usage, I had a credit in my account to cover the cost. Now, that is some real evidence of His provision!

If anyone loves Me, He will obey My teaching. My Father will love him and We will come to him and make our home with him. John 14:23

The lights are on.

And Someone is home.

The Home Church

I had been invited three times.

By the third time, I figured that the Lord was really telling me He wanted me to go. On a Sunday evening, my friend Barb and I went to the "home church" that was meeting in Annville, PA.

A lovely couple, Jim and Carol, greeted us. Casual conversation, introductions and lots of yummy snacks began our evening. There was a nice mix of young and old, with me leaning more toward the old. Carol started us off with some announcements and then passed a basket to help with child care, as well as any needs of the group.

I had $2 in my purse. As the basket passed, I put it in.

Jesus Christ was exalted during the time of worship with singing, praising and honoring the King. He is worthy and the crowd of about twenty-five freely expressed their adoration to Him.

Then Jim shared the message: "Don't Desert in the Desert," right there in the middle of their living room. But it seemed that I was transported into the presence of God. I sensed God speaking directly to me through Jim, as he shared the familiar story of the Israelites in the desert. They were delivered from their bondage in Egypt and were en-route to the promised land. The route could be taken in two weeks. God's plan was to take them there in two years. But because of their disobedience, it took forty years.

Jim asked the question: "How did they get to the wilderness?" They were led there by God and they were sustained there by Him. His presence was with them in the cloud by day and the pillar of fire at night. Jim then gave some reasons for God's delay in our lives that keep us in our own deserts: to prepare us for what He has for us, to increase our dependence on Him, and to have fellowship with Him. Jim encouraged those of us that were in the wilderness due to finances, health issues or troubled relationships, to take full advantage of this time and get beyond any tendencies toward resentment.

After the message, Jim's wife Carol, asked anyone that was in the wilderness to raise their hand. Slowly, I lifted mine. Five or six others did also. Then Carol directed those around us to turn and form small groups to pray for one whose hands were raised. A group of seven was gathered around me when my friend Barb stated, "This is Marti and she has been in the wilderness for a very long time. Her husband left several years ago, she continues to stand for the healing of her family and not only that…she is in a financial wilderness as the real estate market has plunged with the economy." One by one, these dear ones began to pray for me. I wept with their heartfelt concern for me and was humbled by their pleading to the Father on my behalf.

I had an opportunity to share a little of my "desert story" with Jim and Carol before the end of the evening, freely acknowledging that even though this desert time has been long and hard, I would do it again for the intimacy I have gained with the Lord. He had revealed to me at the beginning of the financial downturn that He was working toward the "death of my self-sufficiency." It was a slow, painful and necessary death.

As the meeting came to a close and we were on the way out the door, Carol walked by and dropped an envelope in my purse. Another woman followed suit and placed a check in there. Tears flowed again as I tried to protest, only to hear them say, "This is what we are here for…we are the Body of Christ."

Shocked and deeply grateful I was, when after arriving home, I discovered the gifts to total $800. I wept again. I praised my heavenly Father who, as Jim had shared in the meeting, is who He says He is and does what He says He is going to do…far beyond what I could even think or imagine.

He continued to sustain me in the wilderness.

I felt like I was in the Book of Acts.

All the believers were one in heart and mind. No one claimed that any of his possessions was his own, but they shared everything they had. With great power the apostles continued to testify to the resurrection of the Lord Jesus, and much grace was upon them all. Acts 4:32-33

I heard the Lord proclaim: *"This is My church."*

One Thousand Dollars

It was really cold as I walked in the morning. It was almost Christmas and I was worried. I knew the decline in the real estate market was coming and once again, fear rose up in me. It was almost an hour into my walk and talk with the Lord, belly-aching, really, that my mind shifted.

Finally. I can still see the spot where I was when I made this declaration:

"Really, Lord, I don't know what I am worrying about. You are the God that owns the cattle on a thousand hills. You will take care of me. Why, I could even go to the mailbox today and there could be a check there for $1,000. You could do that. You are God and I don't need to be afraid."

The truth was that I didn't need $1,000 yet…I was just worrying in advance. You know, practicing my fears.

It was a day that I was caring for Nolan and Dylan while Lauren was at the office. The boys had not come long before when the telephone rang. On the other end was the voice of a woman I barely knew, asking if I would be home that day. She wanted to stop by and give me something. Caring for a toddler and a baby was all encompassing for me and I didn't even realize the woman had not come, when the phone rang again around noon. She apologized for not getting there yet and to be honest, by now, I was a bit irritated. I was trying to get ready to go into the office and the boys were awake from their naps and hungry and I had lots to do. She assured me she was almost there and just wanted to drop something off for me.

A few minutes later the doorbell rang. I was holding Dylan in my arms and Nolan was attached at my leg. My hair was still wet and I had no make-up on. I wasn't exactly prepared for company.

The woman at the door was holding a box of Van Winkles Opera

Fudge and an envelope. My first thought was: "Wow, my mother-in-law loves opera fudge and I can save it and re-gift it to her!"

Betty handed me the box and the envelope and said, "The Lord told me to give this to you and even the amount." Puzzled, I just took it from her. That quickly, she was gone.

I walked over to the kitchen island, put the fudge in the refrigerator and curiously opened the envelope. Inside was a Christmas card and a personal check to me for $1,000.

That's right.

ONE THOUSAND DOLLARS.

I started to cry. More tears of disbelief than joy. I just could not figure out what had just happened. The memory of the walk in the morning came back to me. Right at the opening in the trail. Right there when I declared that even today God could have a $1,000 in my mailbox. It was still today. But I didn't even have to go to my mailbox. It came right to my door.

Little Nolan looked up at me and said, "Grandma, why are you crying?"

I couldn't answer. My knees were weak. The phone rang again.

It was Betty.

I couldn't talk. I was still sobbing.

She just kept saying, "I know. I know."

It was later that night when I connected with a mutual friend and got Betty's e-mail address. I just had to tell her the "rest of the story." Funny thing was, as we communicated over the next few days, she had to tell me the "rest of her story."

It was several weeks of feeling a nudge from the Lord. First, Betty heard this: *"Marti Evans might need some help."* And she thought she should send me $250.

Then she forgot about it.

A couple more days went by when she heard again: *"Marti could use some help."* She considered sending me $500.

Then she forgot about it.

But on this morning, she heard the Lord say: *"Write Marti a check for $1,000."*

And she did. And I was blessed beyond measure.

He taught me so much through that...

He will take care of me. He speaks to His children. He uses us to care for each other.

I was excited to think I had a Christmas gift for my mother-in-law and He wanted to give me so much more.

I would have been so, so grateful for $250. But He gives gifts that far exceed what we can imagine.

I had just made a statement of what He can do – it was not even an official request – and He gave me this quick, direct response. I never asked for the thousand dollars, I just declared that He could provide it.

He brought Betty into my life, who has become a dear friend.

He is God.

And so worthy to be praised.

Now to Him who is able to do immeasurably more than all we ask or imagine, according to His power that is at work within us, to Him be glory in the church and in Christ Jesus throughout all generations, forever and ever. Amen. Ephesians 3:20-21

Mums the Word

Everywhere I looked that fall season, there were beautiful mums.

My favorites were the purple ones. I would head to the local grocery store to pick up a few items and see a festive display. I really wanted to buy two of them for the now-empty pots on the front porch. Having discarded the spent annuals, the pots stood at attention giving a less-than-welcoming greeting.

"Are they a need?" I'd ask myself. I knew that the Lord said He would meet my needs. Somehow, they just weren't in that category so I would repeatedly pass them by.

I took a trip with Shannon and her kids to check out the autumn décor at the Renaissance Faire, where Ryan oversees their creation. I had heard how spectacular they were and was hoping to see them before they were taken down for the season.

It was unbelievable to see the thirty-foot scarecrow, a fire-breathing horse with rider and display after display of colorful autumn offerings. Ryan is so gifted and has found a place to express his talents. It was a joy to see his handiwork!

Later that afternoon, I cared for Lauren's children at their home while she was at the office. Arriving back at my house, I was astounded to see my once-empty pots overflowing with purple mums. They were oversized and far bigger than the four-dollar version that I so wanted to buy. Ryan later confessed to planting them.

Not only had the Lord so miraculously met my *needs*, but on this day, He met my *want*. He granted my desire.

Delight yourself in the Lord and He will give you the desires of your heart. Psalm 37:4

777

Impossible.

But true.

Lauren urged me to call her father-in-law.

"Maybe he can help you, Mom."

I was $30,000 in debt from trying to keep the real estate business afloat. I had no income and no prospects. And no idea how I was ever going to even pay the mortgage, let alone the other debts. Matt is a Vice President of one of our local banks.

So I humbled myself.

"Could you help me, Matt?"

Before I could even get out all the details, Matt told me that he could re-finance the mortgage and the other debts into one loan for thirty years, with a fixed rate of 5 percent interest.

"But Matt, you don't understand…I have no income and I am not sure when I will."

He told me to call Dennis and meet with him and he would take care of it. A few days later, I sat with all my information and Dennis just kept shaking his head. "I have never seen a loan go through with these ratios…someone must be looking out for you."

I assured him that Someone was.

Dennis called the next day to let me know that the loan was approved and I could settle at the end of the week.

"What was my credit score?" I asked.

"777."

"Oh my!" I laughed, "God's perfect number!"

And so I settled the loan. Little did I know it would be another eleven months before God supplied a position for me. My new payment was $100 less than my old mortgage payment alone.

Impossible.

But true.

And my God will meet all your needs according to His glorious riches in Christ Jesus. Philippians 4:19

This Qualifies as a Miracle

The return to Pennsylvania was a bit unsettling. The original plan was to be in Hawaii for up to two years, so the necessary but unexpected departure was riddled with uncertainty. I had given up my employment to move to Hawaii to care for my grandchildren, rented my home and sold my car.

When asked what I was going to do by concerned friends and family, I responded that I was going to trust God and watch Him do what He says He will do as I believe *Matthew 6:33*. "His Word is true," was my confident response, though there were definitely moments of not-so-much confidence as I looked at my circumstances. I needed a vehicle. I needed a place to live. I needed a source of income. I had no idea where to start…each seemed to hinge on the other.

But seek first His kingdom and His righteousness, and all these things will be given to you as well. Therefore, do not worry about tomorrow, for tomorrow will worry about itself. Each day has enough trouble of its own. Matthew 6:33-34

My gracious daughters and their families squeezed me into their homes and in seeking the Lord, I determined to start a search for a vehicle, based on a $2,000 budget.

A trip to a local car dealer resulted in bitter disappointment. Apparently, $2,000 buys stinky vehicles with cigarette-burned seats and a really bad paint job in the 150,000 mileage range. My daughter, Shannon, didn't even want me to test drive them, stating that surely God had something better for me.

I had asked my ex-husband to look at the car, once I chose one. When I texted him that the trip to the car dealer was a bust, he suggested that I look at a local garage that used to service our cars. He always took care of the vehicles, so I wasn't aware that they sold cars, but thought it was a great idea. I looked on their website and there were six or seven vehicles listed between $10,000 to $12,000, and one little white Ford Taurus for $2,800.

Shannon went with me the next morning to test drive the Taurus. My ex-husband looked at it that evening and I arrived back at the garage a few days later to purchase it. I wrote a check for $2,800 and drove the car and the salesman to the title transfer company about ten minutes away. We easily chatted on the way, with him doing most of the talking. When we reached our destination, he turned and asked me if I was still living with my husband. He continued to say that he remembered him from when we had our vehicles serviced there years ago.

God opened my mouth. I told of my ex-husband leaving our family, but leaving Jesus first. On the drive back to the garage, the salesman asked what I was doing now. I told of my unexpected return from Hawaii, and His Word to me in *Matthew 6:33*. "My desire is to continue to minister with those women God brings to me, to encourage and help them walk through the excruciating pain God's way," I explained.

When we arrived, he cleaned the "For Sale" sticker off the car for me. He then went into his office, returned and said, "Here, I am giving this back to you."

Into my hand, he placed the check I had given to him earlier.

For $2,800.

I gasped. I protested. I wept.

He insisted that I needed it more than he did. He stated that I was working for God. And God's heart is always to heal. He wanted me to have it back. And he vowed to be praying for my ex-husband.

As I drove away in complete shock, the Lord whispered to me: *"Marti, you are seeking first My kingdom and I am giving you all the things you need. Wait until you see what I do next."*

Great is the Lord and most worthy of praise; His greatness no one can fathom. Psalm 145:3

The Widow's Oil

I really didn't want to file for public assistance for my heat. Friends and family urged me, stating that is what it is for. And the reality was that I had no income and no idea when I would. And how did I get here anyway?

Self-condemnation comes very easily for me…

I heard the Lord interrupt: *"Have you read the Book of Job lately? There are things going on in the heavenly realms that you know nothing about. And stop being your own worst comforter. I am your provider and I can do it anyway I want to."*

I went online and filled out all the paperwork.

Soon, papers came in the mail for more information. And I supplied what they asked the best I knew how. Weeks passed. Every time I tried to reach the office, there was no answer.

The oil gauge went down. I added another sweater, turned the thermostat lower and waited. But while I waited, I would remind the Lord and myself that the widow's oil never ran out. The story in *1 Kings 17* became my story. God had instructed Elijah to go Zarephath, telling him that He had told a widow there to supply Elijah with food. The problem was that the widow only had a handful of flour and a little bit of oil in a jug. Elijah assured her that her supplies would not run out.

One morning, I decided to take a trip to the public assistance office to ask if there was anything I could do to speed up the process. I signed my name on the sheet. And waited…and waited…and waited. Two hours later, I was finally escorted into the office of a sweet lady. She reviewed my information, stating that they could not process the request because I was missing one piece of paper. I told her that I did not have it and didn't know where to get it.

Maybe my eyes were misting over.

Maybe she had a compassionate heart.

Maybe God's Word is true.

She told me that because so many weeks had passed and I still had no income and my oil tank was now almost empty, she could re-file the paperwork. I was now in what they considered a "crisis" situation. She filed it right then and the next day the delivery truck came. I was thinking they would just put a little bit in the tank, but after they left, I realized it was filled to the brim!

The delay was actually God's provision for me.

My oil did not run out.

God's Word is true.

...and the jug of oil did not run dry, in keeping with the word of the Lord.
1 Kings 17:16

Pause to Ponder

- Share some reasons why God asks us to tithe.

- Identify some times in your life when you felt you were in a *free fall*, with no net to catch you except your heavenly Father.

- How do you feel when a need is suddenly met in a way that you hadn't planned?

- Have you ever failed to heed the promptings of God's voice? What have you missed out on?

- Is there an area in your life in which God is saying, "Don't desert in the desert?"

- Recall a time that God far exceeded your expectations and gave you a desire, not just met a need.

- What would you need to believe in order to rest in God's provision and His timing? Can you think of a Scripture that would help you?

His Protection

You are my hiding place;
You will protect me from trouble and
surround me with songs of deliverance.

Psalm 32:7

The Shield

Confusion is what I felt. Mostly. My husband had announced the night before that he needed to "find himself." He wasn't happy. He was planning to move out. Nothing I said seemed to change his mind. It certainly wasn't what I had planned or wanted. I walked out the back door the next morning, as usual, and up onto the trail. I walked for a long time. "Just keep moving and maybe by the time I get back to the house, the nightmare will be over," I told myself.

I cried. I questioned. I pondered. I tried to figure out what happened. What did I do? What didn't I do? How could he do this? What will I do now?

On and on it went…

…until I was interrupted.

By myself.

I realized that all these thoughts, all these wonderings, all these questions were rising up in me causing fear. I said to the Lord, "You know me. You know what is going on. You know what will happen. But I am afraid. This heart of mine is so raw, so wounded, so hurt. I really need Your help. Could You please just put a shield over my heart? Because I am afraid that if You don't, bitterness will seep in and my bleeding, broken heart will explode."

When I returned home, I opened to my Bible passage for the day. It was this:

We wait in hope for the Lord; He is our help and our shield. Psalm 33:20

He was. He is. He will be.

My help and my shield.

Fences or Angels?

I had never lived alone.

I lived with my parents and brothers and sisters until I was a senior in high school. It was when the violence escalated that my aunt and uncle took me in to live with them. By the middle of that year, I was sharing an apartment with a friend, working full time and barely finishing school.

The summer after graduation, I was married and for the next twenty-five years, we lived together, raising our three beautiful children. His job took us to many different locations, but always together.

It wasn't until a year and a half after his abrupt departure from our family and the weddings of my two daughters, that I was faced with living alone. Brian had already been assigned to an Air Force base in Fort Walton Beach, Florida.

I didn't want to live alone.

In the months prior to Shannon and Lauren's weddings, planned just two and a half months apart, with receptions in the back yard, I was able to enclose the yard with six-foot fencing. It was a perfect backdrop for the pine trees that would be laced with white, sparkling lights.

Sensing that the days after Lauren's wedding in August might be difficult for me, my sweet sister, JoAnn, suggested a few days away.

I was so grateful.

I wasn't alone. Yet.

As I approached my home on the return trip from the mountains, nestled at the end of a cul-de-sac, alongside a gently flowing stream, and encircled with a stately white-fenced border, I felt the presence of God. I declared out loud, "You have stood Your warrior angels to guard over me and this property. I will not be afraid. You are my protection, even as my earthly protector has gone. You will never leave me."

I will never be alone.

The angel of the Lord encamps around those who fear Him, and He delivers them. Psalm 34:7

Batman

It was so, so hot. We were having an early spring heat wave and I just couldn't bring myself to turn on the air conditioner. So, I had opened up the window in the kitchen, but the screens weren't in yet. Big mistake.

That night, I was jolted out of a sound sleep by a bang. I looked at the clock. 12:04. It sounded like something hit the window. After turning on the light, I glanced over to see something black between the window and the blinds. I thought maybe it was a large moth and grabbed a magazine to swat it, but as I got closer I realized it was a BAT.

Oh my goodness!

I quickly grabbed my comforter and pillow and made a dash out of the bedroom, slamming the door behind me. I decided to sleep on the couch. Morning came. I waited a respectable amount of time, and then called my son-in-law, Ryan. And frantically explained what had happened. Could he come over? Could he help me? I just can't go back in there!

Ryan shortly arrived with gloves, an old shirt and a sly grin on his face. He thoroughly looked through the bedroom, seeing no trace of the bat. He then went into the adjacent bathroom to see the bat calmly perched on the mirror. He took a picture with his phone, wrapped it in the shirt and brought the bat out to the creek at the edge of the property and let it go.

The Lord protects the simplehearted; when I was in great need, He saved me. Psalm 116:6

Simplehearted: honest, open, and straightforward *(dictionary.com)*

I am honestly, openly and straightforwardly afraid of bats.

I am grateful for the superheroes the Lord sends in my great need.

Ryan…my *batman.*

The Naked Man

It was a mid-summer day as I headed out for my walk on the trail. But it was 2:30 in the afternoon instead of my normal walking time of 6:30 in the morning.

The naked man stood behind a small tree. When I noticed him, I gasped. Not a scream, just an audible gasp.

At that, he made a lewd remark.

I pivoted. Most likely, not as gracefully as a ballerina, and headed the other way.

"Jesus!" I cried out, "Jesus!"

Run. I tried to run. A recent issue with my heart misfiring made it somewhat difficult. "Racy, racy heart," I called it and indeed it was.

The kids were always telling me to take my phone with me when I am on the trail and this day I had it with me, waiting for some return business calls.

Trying to run and dial and not sure who to call, I reached my daughter, Lauren, who was at the office. "Help! Call the Cornwall police… on the trail…between the two bridges…a man…naked…I'm trying to run!"

Within two minutes, Chief Harris called my cell phone, "Someone will be there in thirty seconds." And they were.

"Could I describe him? How old? How tall? Did he have a hat on?"

"Maybe 30's or 40's. Maybe six feet tall. No hat. Just naked."

My son-in-law Chris rode up on his bike. Their neighbor came over to watch Nolan and Dylan. We all went back to the tree. The grass was flattened where the naked man had stood, just a few feet from the trail. By this time another officer arrived with his vehicle. Their investigation revealed fresh bike tire tracks heading back to

Cornwall. It appeared the naked man had quickly left the scene and was most likely long gone.

Chief Harris asked if I was okay.

"I am," I responded. "Will you meet me at 6:30 every morning to walk with me?"

Everyone laughed.

Except me.

I have walked this trail for over ten years, sometimes more than once a day. It's where I meet Jesus. I pray. He listens. I cry. He heals. He answers me.

It's where I walk with Jesus…one step at a time.

It's where I met Jesus on this mid-summer day. I cried out His name. He came.

Quickly.

To rescue me.

It's where I will meet Him tomorrow. I will not be afraid.

He rescues me from my powerful enemy, from my foes, who were too strong for me. Psalm 18:17

Thank you, Cornwall police.

Thank you, Lauren.

Thank you, Chris.

Thank You, Jesus.

I am safe.

Fear of man will prove to be a snare, but whoever trusts in the Lord is kept safe. Proverbs 29:25

The Tornado

The power went off around three o'clock in the afternoon. No electric and no phone service. Lauren, Shannon, Clay and I decided to go to the mall in a neighboring county for a little bit, then out for dinner, since we all were without power. None of us bothered to check the local news.

I arrived back home to a dark house, not knowing when the power would come back on. When I woke in the morning, I walked out the back door toward the trail. I was astonished at what I saw as I attempted to maneuver around trees that were uprooted, and I soon realized it was just not possible to take my walk that day. There was so much devastation.

It seemed surreal coming back onto my property. There was not one branch that had fallen in the yard. Seeing all the destruction just a few feet away, it didn't seem possible that there was no damage.

As I came up to the house, I heard the phone ringing. It was my dear friend Dottie, who called me every morning to pray since the day my husband had abruptly left. She wondered if I was okay. I told her about trying to walk on the trail and being unable to get through. She then told me of the F3 tornado that had touched down in my area. Over one hundred homes were destroyed, some just a mile or so away.

Oh my! No, I did not know. In a short time, the electric did come back on and I was able to catch up on the news.

I am amazed at the way God protects me.

The Lord will protect him and preserve his life; He will bless him in the land and not surrender him to the desire of his foes. Psalm 41:2

Superstar Driver

Friday night was the night that everyone was available to go out for dinner to celebrate Reed and Dylan's birthdays. They were born in December, just a year and four days apart and we usually celebrate them together.

Some friends had recently invited me to join them on a Sunday morning at their church and then took me to a buffet for lunch. While there, I mentioned that my quickly growing grand boys would love this place. I decided to start saving to be able to bring their families there for dinner.

The night had finally arrived. No simple feat, coordinating work, school, and sports schedules. We were on our way! It was already dark and a little misty from a recent rainfall as we left at 5:30 p.m. Traffic was heavy as we traveled east on Route 283.

I was in the van with Shannon and Ryan's family. The car in front of us started to brake and Shannon realized she would not be able to stop in time to avoid running into it. She gently swerved to the left onto the shoulder and the car behind us hit the back right side of the van, then slammed into the black pick-up truck that Shannon had avoided hitting. Then, an 18-wheeler smashed into the truck! Everything stopped. We all quickly exited the van, as the large truck, just inches from us, started leaking what looked like fuel. Every vehicle involved had major damage and had to be towed. Except the van we were in.

After the police investigation was complete, we were able to drive from the scene of the accident and make it to the restaurant to celebrate the boys' birthdays.

I was so impressed and grateful for Shannon's calm handling of the situation…she really is a *superstar driver!*

…for He guards the course of the just and protects the way of His faithful ones. Proverbs 2:8

Psalm 91

"Brian, who dwells in the shelter of the Most High will rest in the shadow of the Almighty. Brian will say of the Lord, 'He is my refuge and my fortress, my God, in whom I trust.'

Surely He will save Brian from the fowler's snare and from the deadly pestilence. He will cover Brian with His feathers, and under His wings Brian will find refuge; His faithfulness will be Brian's shield and rampart.

Brian will not fear the terror of night, nor the arrow that flies by day, nor the pestilence that stalks in the darkness, nor the plague that destroys at midday.

A thousand may fall at Brian's side, ten thousand at his right hand, but it will not come near Brian. He will only observe with his eyes and see the punishment of the wicked.

Since Brian makes the Most High his dwelling – even the Lord, who is Brian's refuge – then no harm will befall Brian, no disaster will come near Brian's tent.

For He will command His angels concerning Brian to guard Brian in all his ways; they will lift Brian up in their hands, so that Brian will not strike his foot against a stone.

Brian will tread upon the lion and the cobra; Brian will trample the great lion and serpent.

'Because Brian loves Me,' says the Lord, 'I will rescue him. I will protect him, for Brian acknowledges My name. Brian will call upon Me, and I will answer him; I will be with Brian in trouble, I will deliver him and honor him. With long life will I satisfy Brian and show him My salvation.'"

I have no idea how many times Brian has gone overseas into a war zone to serve our country. But I know this: the very first time he was deployed, the Lord had me revise Psalm 91 with Brian's name in it and send it to friends and family.

I asked them to pray for God's protection over my son.

And He answered.

Answer me when I call to You, O my righteous God. Give me relief from my distress; be merciful to me and hear my prayer. Psalm 4:1

Crash!

It wasn't even the end of October and a snowstorm was brewing. Because of the sharp drop in temperatures, the rains turned to snow and then to ice. All day long, you could hear limbs crashing to the ground throughout the whole neighborhood.

The power went off.

And remained off for five days.

At the end of the patio, we had planted two ornamental pear trees when we moved in several years ago. They grow quickly, but do not have a strong root system. Just a few months before, one of the trees fell over during Hurricane Irene. As the ice was accumulating on the branches, the remaining tree began to bend.

I prayed from the kitchen window, fearful the thirty-foot tree would hit the house.

I anxiously watched as the lone Bradford pear tree split in two, then in three sections. One by one, they crashed to the ground. The first went to the right. The second section fell to the left. Then, the third section went straight down the middle of the yard.

CRASH!

CRASH!

CRASH!

I praised from the kitchen window, thankful the thirty-foot tree didn't hit the house.

But let all who take refuge in You be glad; let them ever sing for joy. Spread Your protection over them; that those who love Your name may rejoice in You. For surely, O Lord, You bless the righteous; You surround them with Your favor as with a shield. Psalm 5:11-12

Surely

Surely: firmly, unerringly, undoubtedly, assuredly, inevitably or without fail, certainly, with confidence, un-hesitantly *(dictionary.com)*

I was pondering the 23rd Psalm, that great psalm that gets read at funerals. As I came upon the last verse, I realized it is really a psalm for the living.

Surely goodness and love will follow me all the days of my life, and I will dwell in the house of the Lord forever. Psalm 23:6

I love the word "surely." So firm. So certain. So *sure*. It absolutely is going to happen.

Now lately as I look behind me, I perceive that what is following me is devastation, destruction, catastrophe, ruin and trouble.

But, it is not so. God's Word is true. And absolute. And sure. If the Lord is my shepherd, and He is, then it is absolutely, for certain that what is following me is good.

Always.

Every day of my life.

Here's the even greater part: that I will dwell in the house, or the presence, of the Lord. Forever. Not just for eternity. But for right now.

Dictionary.com states that a related phrase for surely is "sure as shooting."

So here's my paraphrase of *Psalm 23:6.*

Sure as shooting, that is goodness and love coming right up behind me, not destruction and evil, because the Lord is my shepherd and right now, this very minute, I am living in His presence. And not just for this moment.

For forever.

Though I walk in the midst of trouble, You preserve my life; You stretch out Your hand against the anger of my foes, with Your right hand You save me. Psalm 138:7

Covered

I don't understand. I really don't. But I have come to trust.

Many years after my husband left, divorced me, married another woman and divorced again, I lived in close proximity to him. This man, who seemed to love Jesus at one time, was now steeped in his addictions, following after other gods and just plain mean.

What happened? How could one I thought I knew be so very different than I understood him to be? It's a fearful thing to watch. So many questions…

As I have wandered in the wilderness, I have come to know my God who says:

The fear of the Lord is the beginning of knowledge, but fools despise wisdom and discipline. Proverbs 1:7

The Lord is a gentleman. He will not force Himself on anyone. We love Him in response to His love for us and He would rather die than live without us. And He did.

For God so loved the world that He gave His one and only Son, that whoever believes in Him shall not perish, but have eternal life. John 3:16

We love because He first loved us. 1 John 4:19

I have come to know that my God is a good God, so good that He has kept me safe. I have seen His hand on my life, as I walk with Him. He loves me and I see that love lived out in His protection of me.

The Lord will keep you from all harm — He will watch over your life; the Lord will watch over your coming and going both now and forevermore. Psalm 121:7-8

I don't understand.

But I trust Him.

Pause to Ponder

- In what ways do you attempt to control circumstances to protect yourself rather than trusting God in your journey?

- When have you been afraid? How did you respond to that feeling?

- Have you ever been bitter toward God or others? Ask the Lord to forgive you and shield your heart so that it remains soft and responsive to the Spirit.

- What types of walls have you built around your heart to protect yourself from pain, heartache, abandonment and fear?

- Has there been a time when you felt that God has not come through for you?

- Who in your life has God used to show you His help and protection?

- Has God ever asked you to do something scary? How did He help you to feel safe?

- Describe a time when you clearly sensed God's protection.

- Is there a situation that you have been faced with that you have given up the need to understand and come to surrender in trust to God?

His Power

*The Son is the radiance of God's glory
and the exact representation of His being,
sustaining all things by His powerful word.*

Hebrews 1:3

Emergency!

I was at the local youth ministry building where I served on the Board of Directors. Several of us were gathering there to pray. As I waited in the parking lot for the rest of the group to arrive, I looked through the mail I had just picked up from the post office.

My mortgage payment of $750 was due in a few days and I was down to $500 in my bank account. I could not imagine how I was going to pay the bill. As I opened the mail, there was an envelope from a friend that contained a check for $250.

I sat there stunned, yet knowing that my God had just come through. Even as I recognized His goodness and His perfect timing, I felt uncertain of what to do. To drain my whole savings would mean that I had nothing left. I cried out to Him, "Should I take all this to pay the mortgage? What if something happens? What if there is an emergency?"

He cried right back to me: *"Your life is an emergency. And that is exactly how I want it."*

I had to laugh. He can be so *blunt,* so *truth*-speaking, so *clear* in His instruction to me. This God of mine, who has proven Himself over and over, needed to remind me again of His power toward me, His beloved daughter.

It is He, who teaches me to pray.

Give us each day our daily bread. Luke 11:3

It is He, who tells me about tomorrow.

Do not boast about tomorrow, for you do not know what a day may bring forth. Proverbs 27:1

It is He, who takes care of me in the wilderness.

During the forty years that I led you through the desert, your clothes did not wear out, nor did the sandals on your feet...I did this so that you might know that I am the Lord your God. Deuteronomy 29:5-6

My life is an emergency and that's exactly how I want it.

One Yellow Rose

People who love me send me yellow roses. They are my favorite. Many events of my life have been celebrated with this beautiful flower.

In the early morning hours of January 3rd, in shock after hearing of the sudden death of my beloved Aunt Barbara, I prayed. I asked God to give me the assurance that she was with Him. These words from *Matthew 7:7-8* were part of my readings for the day:

Ask and it will be given to you; seek and you will find; knock and the door will be opened to you. For everyone who asks receives; he who seek finds; and to him who knocks, the door will be opened.

I knew with certainty that He heard my prayer and He would answer. I never would have imagined how.

At the cemetery after the funeral, we were handed flowers to place on Barbara's casket. I was one of the last ones to place mine. I noticed that in an array of red roses, lilacs, white spider mums and carnations, there was only one yellow rose. Not realizing I said it aloud, "I love yellow roses, they're my favorite." My niece Jill turned to me and said, "I love them, too."

The next morning, I walked along the Rails to Trails, my set-apart time to be with Jesus. I asked for His presence and comfort for all of my family and again, that I would know Barbara was with Him.

On the way back to the house, as I was passing a bench placed on the side of the trail, I saw it.

One yellow rose.

Only one, it was laying across the back of the bench. In the barrenness of a cold winter day, one live yellow rose. I carried it home, weeping all the way, thanking God for answering my prayer.

The words spoken at the funeral rang in my ears:

I am the way and the truth and the life. No one comes to the Father except through Me. John 14:6

People who love me send me yellow roses.

Thank You, Jesus.

Thank you, Barbara.

I love You, too.

A Charge to the Bride

It wasn't long after Chris and Lauren were engaged that Lauren asked me to give the "Charge to the Bride" at their wedding ceremony. Chris' Dad agreed to do the "Charge to the Groom." I had seen it done at a few weddings and it is really a beautiful gift of wisdom and experience that parents pass on to their children, to encourage them to have a successful marriage.

This was the last thing I felt qualified to do. My marriage was in the throes of destruction and I was powerless in myself to do anything about it. What advice could I possibly give?

The more I objected, the more Lauren assured me that God would give me the words to say. I fully committed it to Him.

On the morning of the wedding, I had the document open on the computer, still unsure what I was to share in a few short hours. Brian apparently read it and as he passed me in the kitchen said, "It's good Mom." I felt God's assurance in my son's words.

I was nervous. I had not had occasion to speak in public before, let alone in front of two hundred guests on this most special day in my daughter's life.

Here is the "Charge to the Bride."

"My dear, dear Lauren,

I am humbled to stand before you on this dream-filled day!

Not long after your college graduation, great sorrow struck your young life – not once, but several times. It seemed you could hardly catch your breath and you were struck down again. And as your Mom, I prayed that I could take that pain for you. But we both found out, life just doesn't work that way.

In the Book of Matthew, Jesus talks about the wide road that leads to destruction and the narrow road that leads to life. In your deep suffering, you could have rebelled and taken that road of seeking comfort in alcohol or drugs or bad relationships. But instead, you turned to God and let Him walk you through the pain on that narrow road.

When I was just a little younger than you are today, I was rocking your baby sister in my rocking chair and listening to the radio. I heard a message that changed my life. I heard that Jesus loved me so much that He took all my sin and shame and died on a cross so I could be forgiven, so I could be free, so I could live forever with Him. And I accepted that precious gift.

Soon after that, God put it in my heart to pray, not only for my children, but for their spouses as well. So for over twenty years I have prayed for Chris, not knowing his name, only his Creator.

I will never forget that Saturday morning when Mr. Grumbine, the florist, rang the doorbell carrying a beautiful bouquet of yellow roses. I brought them into your room. We cried and prayed together because we knew that God had just answered prayer. You often told me that the first man to send you a dozen yellow roses was the man you were going to marry. But, Chris didn't know that. Only you and I and God knew. Just a few weeks later, Chris asked for permission to marry you.

Today, God has given you the desire of your heart. He has given you Christopher Michael Groff – a faithful, honorable man of character and integrity, who treasures you and loves you with his whole heart.

My encouragement to you today, Lauren, is to stay on that narrow road. You will be tempted at times to take the wide road. But make the commitment to God and each other to stay on that narrow road that leads to life.

I love you, Lauren and Chris, and I pray God's richest blessings on you."

When I finished, I looked up. Many tears were falling and it was seriously silent.

Chris' Dad broke the ice when he said, "I should have gone first!"

The congregation laughed.

Many comments were made in the receiving line, and I praise God that His power was seen through the tender story of His amazing confirmation of Lauren's covenant husband.

Therefore I will boast all the more gladly about my weaknesses, so that Christ's power may rest on me. 2 Corinthians 12:9

A Supernatural Bubble

I didn't really want to sell my vehicle. I really liked it. But, it was in the real estate company name, and in order to transfer it to me personally, it would cost me almost $1,000 in taxes. It may as well have been a million.

I knew I had to have it inspected before I could sell it, so I took my Honda CRV to the local dealer, where I usually had its maintenance done. While there, I explained my situation to the manager. What I wanted to do was to trade in my CRV, get a less expensive car and have a little bit of cash to live on until I secured a new position. So, that meant I was looking to purchase a good, used car for around $9,000.

"Not too likely," he declared.

"But I know that God can work it out for me," I humbly responded.

I was assigned to Don, a used car salesman.

Don wasn't too hopeful either.

"What kind of car do you want?"

"How much do you want to spend?"

"What color do you want it to be?"

I seriously could not answer that last question. Was I really going to have a choice of color?

So Don started his search. I came in to look at a gray-blue Honda Civic with really high mileage. I never bought a used car by myself, and before I could have someone else look at it, it was sold, so I lost that one.

A week later, I came to a stop sign and said out loud, "I think Don will call today and the car will be red. I would like to have a red car again." I didn't think I could have a preference of color, so it surprised me when I said it.

I had told Don the best place to reach me was my cell number, although I had given him my office and home numbers, as well. All day, I kept wondering if Don was going to call. I had even driven by the dealership and thought about stopping in, but didn't. When I arrived home, there was a message on the answering machine from Don. I wasn't surprised. He had found a car that I may want to look at...call him. Then I went right over with Lauren to help me make the decision, there was a red Honda Accord with less miles on it than my CRV!

Decision made.

I bought it, and after the trade-in, deposited a little over $5,000 into my account.

The day I signed the paperwork and picked up the car will forever be engraved on my mind. There was my shiny "new" red car on display in the showroom. Don was bending down to put on the new license plate and making small talk.

"So, are you going to stay in real estate?"

I responded that I will do whatever God leads me to do, but I hope it is not real estate.

"What do you want to do?"

"Well, I have a couple of books floating around in my head."

"About what?"

"One is about wandering in the wilderness. I've been doing that for a long time. The other one can't be written yet. It's called: *Healed, Whole and Home Again.*"

Then, I shared a little of my story with him.

I thought Don was going to drop the license plate.

He went on to tell me his story. He was a pastor for twenty-two years when his wife declared that she no longer wanted to be married. While he spoke and shared some of the details, I felt that although we were standing in the middle of the showroom, the Lord had enveloped us in a bubble. I sensed people moving about us and yet felt completely encased in the love and presence of God. He had put us together for "such a time as this." Don stated that he was believing God for the healing of his family. Before he sent me off in my "new" Accord, he prayed the most beautiful, heartfelt plea to the Father on behalf of our families. What an awesome God!

Great is our Lord and mighty in power; His understanding has no limit.
Psalm 147:5

What's Too Hard

I just happened to be home on Wednesday afternoon, March 22nd, quickly running the vacuum, when I heard the persistent ring of the telephone. It was my daughter-in-law, Amanda, hardly able to speak from the excitement of the phone call she had just received.

Brian and Amanda had contracted with an adoption agency in California, where they were currently living, just six weeks prior. For many years, Amanda suffered the painful effects of endometriosis and was told she wouldn't be able to conceive. They had recently celebrated their second anniversary and were anxious to start a family.

The adoption agency told them that it would most likely be two years until they were matched. They were hopeful the baby would be born in California. If he was, they could possibly be there for the birth, and then take the baby home with them from the hospital a few days later. Any other location in the United States could mean waiting up to three weeks, depending on the state laws. That meant an extended stay in a hotel, until everything was finalized and they were cleared to cross state lines.

Lisa, their adoption facilitator, had just called. They were chosen by a birth mom, and in only three weeks, she was due and the baby was a little boy! The two year anticipated wait was only a month and a half.

But, there was more news...

"Guess, guess where the baby will be born!" Amanda gushed.

"California," I replied, knowing that was their desire.

"No. Pennsylvania. And not just Pennsylvania. Lebanon, Pennsylvania. At the very same hospital where all your other grand boys were born!"

How could that even be possible? Of all the places in the United States, my newest grandson was going to be born right here!

And he was. Just one week later, on March 29th, Trevor James was born. I was honored to be able to hold him just one day later, as Brian and Amanda made their way across the country to meet their firstborn.

Instead of a three week stay in a hotel, they were able to stay with me, where I had a room set up for grandkid visits and a guest room. What a joy those weeks were as we celebrated the miracle of Trevor's arrival!

Nine months later, right before Christmas, another excited phone call came. This time, Brian and Amanda were on the line.

"Are you sitting down?"

"Yes."

"We're pregnant."

"What?!?! But, that's impossible!"

On my birthday, August 3rd, Parker John was born.

What's too hard for God?

NOTHING.

Great is the Lord and most worthy of praise; His greatness no one can fathom. One generation will commend Your works to another; they will tell of Your mighty acts. They will speak of the glorious splendor of Your majesty, and I will meditate on Your wonderful works. They will tell of the power of Your awesome works, and I will proclaim Your great deeds. Psalm 145:3-6

The Migraine

A woman called into the chiropractic office, where I was working part-time, in deep distress, suffering from a migraine. She had been in for an adjustment the night before and had taken special medication, but nothing was working. The doctor suggested that she come in again, so I scheduled her for later that evening.

After her appointment, she spoke with me at the check-out counter. She was obviously still in great pain. She told me a little of her story, then with tears in her eyes stated, "I need a miracle."

I looked into her sad, pained eyes and said, "Well, let's ask God for one."

I gently laid my hand on her head as she closed her eyes. I quietly prayed, "Jesus, we are asking You for a miracle. You have said that You are the healer. We are asking You to be for this woman who You said You are. In Jesus' name. Amen."

She thanked me as she walked out.

It was several hours later when Steph, the office manager, told me that the woman had called in to say she was feeling much better.

Praise God.

Jesus is indeed the healer.

Praise the Lord, O my soul, and forget not all His benefits - who forgives all your sins and heals all your diseases, who redeems your life from the pit and crowns you with love and compassion, who satisfies your desires with good things so that your youth is renewed like the eagle's. Psalm 103:2-5

It's a…Girl?

The recent events had everyone, including Dr. Peggy, prepared to welcome a little boy into the world. With the baby's diagnosis of cysts on the right kidney, the decision was made to induce labor for Lauren almost three weeks early. She and Chris had agreed shortly into the pregnancy to not find out the sex of the baby. It really didn't matter. A third boy would be fun and a girl would be a thrill, but after having their last baby die in the womb, what really mattered is that the baby would live.

The discussion with Dr. Peggy about the plan they were formulating to bring the baby early, included her mentioning whether or not to do the circumcision right away. It raised a question in Lauren's mind as to why Dr. Peggy was letting them know the baby was a boy when they had asked not to find out. The next day the whole family, with Nolan and Dylan in tow, stopped in at Dr. Peggy's office and she told the boys they were going to have a new brother. With that said, everyone was sure the baby was a boy. Somehow it seemed that Dr. Peggy had forgotten that Chris and Lauren didn't want to know the sex of the baby.

With the recent enlarging of the baby's kidney, once again the sex really didn't matter, so everyone prepared for a boy. "My three sons" was what I thought and maybe someday, Lauren would be pregnant again and God would grant her the sweet desire of her heart, to have a daughter.

The laboring was not easy. Twenty-three hours long with a migraine headache that was impossible for Lauren to bear, which impeded medication to speed things up. So long; so hard. All the paperwork was filled out in blue for a boy, all the nurses were ready, when suddenly, in a matter of five minutes, Lauren dilated from five to ten centimeters and out came…a *girl!* Stunned, shocked, in disbelief were the nurses, Dr. Peggy and Lauren and Chris.

Upon further discussion, Dr. Peggy explained that she thought it was Lauren who told her it was a boy, but in reality she never had. Oh my! So, why not stun everyone else? Chris made the calls, announcing the baby's arrival, and declaring they were going to share their new baby's name when everyone came to the hospital. Well, that was at 5:00 a.m. I had to wait for Nolan and Dylan to wake up, so I showered, e-mailed, Face-booked, then called who I needed to, sharing that the baby was here and it was a boy!

Chris' parents made their phone calls, as well. Imagine my surprise when Nolan went into the hospital room first, then told me the baby's name was *Alison*. Now, that didn't sound like a boys' name. Then it registered. I looked at Lauren and then Chris and heard them say, "It's a *girl!*"

There was Jenny, their nurse, tending the baby. I insisted she take off the diaper so I could see for myself.

Indeed, Alison is a *girl!* 7 lbs,7 oz; 20 inches long. Born August 1st, 2010 at 4:47 a.m. Perfectly and powerfully formed by the hand of God.

For You created my inmost being; You knit me together in my mother's womb. I praise You because I am fearfully and wonderfully made; Your works are wonderful, I know that full well. Psalm 139:13-14

Heaven is for Real

It was 6:00 p.m. when I came back to the hospital. Having arrived the night before at about midnight, I was in desperate need of sleep and a shower, so I took a break earlier in the afternoon and headed to my sister JoAnn's home. Upon entering the hospital room, I was surprised to find only my sisters; Marylee, JoAnn and her daughter Joyce sitting by Mom. The room had been bustling with brothers, sisters, nieces and nephews earlier in the day and now it was noticeably quiet. I settled in a chair on the right of Mom's bed, JoAnn was on the left, Joyce was at the foot of the bed and Marylee was to the side.

We comfortably chatted with each other, with a dying Mom between us.

Perhaps it was the gold scarf. I had told of my friend that I had just visited a few days before who was battling cancer. She was sporting the most adorable pink scarf...I said I wish we had a scarf for Mom. Joyce, replied that she had one in the car that JoAnn had put in her stocking for Christmas. She went out to the car to retrieve it and lovingly tied it around Mom's neck. Joyce didn't think it looked so good with Mom's pasty, paling skin. I thought it complemented her silver hair.

Perhaps it was the photos that my brother, John, had brought to the hospital earlier in the day, many we had never seen before, of Mom and Dad in their younger years, in their prime. Before Dad's brain cyst. Happier times. We spoke of how beautiful Mom was in her wedding dress and how very handsome Dad looked. That gold scarf sure made Mom look ready to meet her husband again.

Perhaps it was the story I shared of visiting Mom on Christmas Eve, six weeks prior. I read her the book *Heaven is For Real For Kids* by Todd Burpo. I had brought it along to give her. The book tells of Todd's three-year-old son Colton's trip to heaven. While he was there, he met his big sister, who had been an earlier miscarriage. He also met his grandfather, who died before Colton was born. He met

Jesus and recounted how much Jesus loved the children. The pictures in the book are stunning and biblically accurate and I believe it brought great comfort to Mom. As I was reading to her, Mom's face lit up and her eyes glistened, when I told of Colton meeting his sister in heaven. I had said, "Mom, you had two miscarriages and you will meet your babies in heaven!"

Perhaps it was the story about Dylan, my five-year-old grandson. The night before, as we were finishing up our Valentine's party, the phone rang. The caller was my brother, Stephen, telling me that Mom was on her way to the hospital and it didn't look good. Eversensitive Dylan noticed I was upset. I told him that Uncle Stephen called to tell me that Mimi was going to the hospital and she may die soon and go to heaven. His entire body perked up and with a huge grin, he exclaimed, "the streets there are gold!"

Perhaps it was the conversation we had about the walls in heaven that are full of jewels. And that there is no sun, for God is all the light we need. We surmised that it is warm in heaven and Mom would like that. She hated to be cold.

Perhaps it was that split second realization when JoAnn blurted out, "Mom will see Gregory!" Beautiful, precious Gregory, JoAnn and Tim's tiny baby, who suddenly died at the age of four months. Mom's grandbaby.

Perhaps it was *all* of what we were comfortable chatting about, with Mom between us.

It was at the moment when JoAnn said Gregory's name that the four of us simultaneously turned to see Mom...exhale one last breath.

Then she was gone. To heaven. Where the streets are gold and the walls are jeweled and there is no sun, but it is always light and warm, and Mom met Dad and their two babies and Gregory and Jesus, who said to her: *Well done, good and faithful servant! Matthew 25:21*

Now I know that the Lord saves His anointed; He answers him from His holy heaven with the saving power of His right hand. Psalm 20:6

Soul Trauma

I wasn't sure if I would ever recover.

It was the end of the evening appointments, just a few minutes before we were finished for the day. Hannah, Dr. Paul's daughter, asked if she could leave a few minutes early. She and her brother, Jeff, wanted to get to the hospital to visit their grandfather, who just recently had a heart attack. Dr. Paul, Hannah and Jeff lived in one of the apartments above the office. Since the last patient had already arrived, I told Hannah to just go. I would finish up.

Within minutes, Hannah returned. She calmly told me to get her dad, who was still in the examination room with the last patient. I could tell she was shaken. She continued to say, "Jeff is in the tub and there is blood all over."

Immediately, I got Dr. Paul, stating that he needed to come right away.

The next several hours evolved like a horror movie. Phone calls. Ambulances. Police. Investigators. Up and down the steps to the apartment.

Shock. Disbelief. Prayer. Weeping.

At some point in the three hours prior to Hannah's discovery, Jeff had taken a gun, gotten into the tub and shot himself.

The ambulance that came, left without him.

When I finally left the office several hours later, having done all I could do, I drove back to my house in Cornwall. My empty house, with an empty heart, not quite knowing how to process all that had just occurred.

I was able to reach each of my daughters and we talked for a little bit. Then, I contacted my son through Facetime. Brian has been exposed to the horrors of war. He let me tell him what had happened. He listened. He prayed with me. And he told me to keep talking about it. That's how the trauma to my soul would heal.

The days and weeks and months that followed were critical. At work, I would go into the back hallway to do some cleaning of the building, and have a flashback. Like it was happening all over again.

Slowly, slowly, as I kept talking about it, walking alongside Dr. Paul and Hannah in their grief, seeking God, He did begin to heal the trauma to my soul.

My soul clings to You; Your right hand upholds me. Psalm 63:8

The Journal

We arrived at the Olive Tree Hotel in Jerusalem following the long airplane flight and short bus ride. Susan, a team member for Michael Card's Journey to Israel tour, handed each of us a bag and a key to our rooms. Carol and I headed to the elevator, ready to unpack and relax before dinner.

When I opened the bag and saw the rich, brown leather journal, I immediately wondered what I was going to do with it. I love journals, I write in one pretty much every day. But they never look like this. Mine are the composition-style notebooks from the Dollar Store. I never use fancy journals. I don't write fancy. I write raw and real and raging, sometimes. If I used a journal like this, I'd have to use nice, sweet, gentle words. At least, that's how it felt to me. So, I just put the journal on top of my suitcase and forgot about it.

We were several days into the tour when I heard the nudging voice of the Lord say, *"I want you to ask men to bless you. Ask them to write in your journal."* Well, that was so far out of my comfort zone, I nudged right back, "I can't. Men don't bless me. Men curse me. All my life they've cursed me. I can't." Which, of course, He was completely aware of. Being the perfect gentleman that He is, He didn't respond. But over and over for the next few days, He nudged and nudged and nudged me. And over and over for the next few days, I said, "I can't."

I knew God had me there in Israel for a very special reason. Maybe it was more than one reason. I was there, against all odds. He brought me there, that I knew. I did not and could not get there any other way. My heart, my life, my whole being wants to serve Him, honor Him and love Him…He has done so much for me. So, finally, I responded. He had made it perfectly clear who I was to ask to bless me. Three different men.

It was day seven of the ten-day tour. I brought the journal with me to dinner, thinking that if David, our tour guide, sat at the same table I did, I would ask him to bless me and write in my journal. When I came back from the buffet, there was David, sitting at the table! I had the journal right next to my silverware. We all chatted easily and then David pointed to the journal and asked if it was a Bible. He needed to get the verses together for the next day's itinerary. "No," I said, "it's my journal and I wanted to talk to you about it." He nodded and promptly left to go find a Bible.

The next day, as Carol and I left the hotel room, I stuffed the journal into my backpack. It wasn't getting any easier, anticipating the moment I would actually ask men to bless me, as God was so clearly instructing me. I rehearsed it in my head, so no one would get the wrong impression. I was going to say, "Could we please have a private conversation in a public place?" Really, it was the strangest, most difficult, nonsensical thing. Who does this? Who asks men to bless them? And if God really wanted men to bless me, couldn't He just ask them Himself? He is God and He certainly could do that, but for some reason He had me intimately involved in the process.

The next morning, David had just finished a short re-cap about the Wailing Wall. He had his headset on and we all had our earphones in, so we could hear him directly over the crowds and the noise from the wind. He invited us to go to the Wailing Wall if we wanted to, and meet back at the bus in twenty minutes or so. It was time. I walked over to David, first asking if his headset was off. He flipped it up and nodded. I surely didn't want this crazy conversation to be broadcast to the whole group!

My practice paid off. I calmly asked, "David, could we please have a private conversation in a public place?" His response wasn't in my plan. "Sure, now is a good time. Let's go over here." He was pointing to a fenced area, maybe fifteen feet away. I was thinking we were going to make an appointment to meet later. I hadn't planned what I was going to say next.

Over to the fence we went. I took the beautifully bound brown book out of my backpack and handed it to him. I told David of receiving it and wondering what I was to do with it. I write all the time, in ninety-nine cent journals. It was too fancy. I told him of God's nudging. I told him God wanted me to ask men to bless me. I told him that men do not bless me. They curse me. I asked if he would please take it and write something in it and bless me. And I said it very fast, because I was very afraid.

The face of David turned into the face of Jesus right in front of my eyes. Compassion. Pure, holy compassion. David said, "Marti, I am so sorry men have cursed you and abused you and hurt you. That is not God's design. He wants men to bless women and care for them. Yes, I will write in your journal. But, may I bless you right now?" That also wasn't in my script.

So, right there, in Jerusalem, in the courtyard, in front of the Wailing Wall, David reached out his hand toward me and said these words. His Word:

The Lord bless you and keep you; the Lord make His face shine upon you and be gracious to you; the Lord turn His face toward you and give you peace. Numbers 6:24-26

Then I went to the Wailing Wall and wept. And wailed.

David returned the journal the next day. I asked the other two men to sign it. On the plane ride back to the United States, God began to reveal His purpose of such a strange assignment. As I read what each one wrote in the journal, God made it clear to me.

One wrote a father blessing. One wrote a husband blessing. One wrote a brother blessing.

The very men that had cursed, abused, abandoned and hurt me. God used the words of these men to overturn that curse and bless me instead. Oh, the lengths that the Lord will go to heal! He *is* the healer and He loves me.

However, the Lord your God would not listen to Balaam but turned the curse into a blessing for you, because the Lord your God loves you. Deuteronomy 23:5

Pause to Ponder

- The greatest power ever displayed is the death and resurrection of Jesus Christ. What have you done with the offer of eternal life through the sacrifice of God's Son? Have you experienced His salvation in your life? Share your story.

- Tell of an account from the Old or New Testament when God displayed His power. Can you recall a time from your own life when you have experienced His power?

- What resources does God give us to get through a tough situation?

- Did you ever trust His power to resurrect you from a seemingly "dead" situation? What was the outcome?

- Has God ever turned a "curse" into a "blessing" for you?

- There are so many stories in the Bible of God doing impossible things. Describe a time when God did for you what seemed "impossible."

- Share about something you specifically prayed for and how God answered.

His Promises

God is not a man, that He should lie,
nor a son of man, that He should change His mind. Does
He speak and then not act?
Does He promise and not fulfill?

Numbers 23:19

The Blind Man

I was near the sugar-white beaches in Fort Walton Beach, Florida, trying to make sense of it all.

I flew down to be with Brian, just three weeks after my husband's abrupt exit from our family. It was the week we had set aside to celebrate our 25th wedding anniversary in Jamaica. I wasn't in Jamaica. Instead, I knew I needed to be with my son in his grief.

The night my husband made his confession, he made some declarations.

"I am an adulterer. I am a womanizer. I am a liar."

I couldn't quite grasp it. By all accounts, he was a family man, doting on our children, attending their activities, driving them to and fro... far more than I did. A good man. A good husband. A good father.

"This is the real me," he declared when I showed obvious confusion at his announcement.

When the fog cleared a bit, I began to ask the Lord this question:

"How do You see him?"

Brian, stationed at the local Air Force Base, left early every morning for work. While he was gone, I spent much time with the Lord, praying and reading His Word and expecting His answer.

I love those who love Me, and those who seek Me find Me. Proverbs 8:17

And I did.

In my scheduled reading in *Mark 8*, the Word was illuminated and the Lord directly answered my question.

It was the story of a blind man. Now, there are several stories of blind men in the Bible. But this day, this blind man was His message just for me.

They came to Bethsaida, and some people brought a blind man and begged Jesus to touch him. He took the blind man by the hand and led him outside the village. When He had spit on the man's eyes and put His hands on him, Jesus asked, "Do you see anything?" He looked up and said, "I see people, they look like trees walking around." Once more Jesus put His hands on the man's eyes. Then his eyes were opened, his sight was restored, and he saw everything clearly. Jesus sent him home. Mark 8:22-26

I sensed the Lord's direct answer to the question:

"How do You see him?"

"He is blind. But that is not how I created him. I created him to love Me, love you, love his children, nurture and care for them. I did not create him to be an adulterer, a womanizer or a liar. That is the work of the evil one. He has blinded him. And I want you to keep praying for him. I touched him once and he came home. But he never came home to Me. He was still confused about what he was seeing. He saw your marriage as a burden and not the blessing that I intended it to be. I will touch him again. And when I do…he will have the veil of deception removed from his eyes. He will see Me again and all I have done for him and all I want for him."

In the quietness of that empty apartment, I clearly heard the voice of the Lord.

When Brian returned from his work day, I shared this with him. I felt my calling at that moment. *Healed, Whole and Home Again* was birthed in my heart that afternoon. I had no idea how to write a book. I only knew that He had planted it for a time to come. He will:

Touch him a second time.

Open his blinded eyes. Restore his sight. And send him back to Jesus.

He is teaching me to walk with Him…one step at a time.

The Rescue

It was the third morning after the abrupt and unexpected exit of my husband from our home. It was very difficult to get ready and out of the house to go to the office. I was grabbing onto the sink top in the bathroom, looking into the mirror at my red-rimmed swollen eyes, crying out loud, "God, I am desperate for You! I need help! Help! Help me!"

Right then, the doorbell rang.

And rang. Quickly. Urgently.

Not once, but over and over again. I pulled myself together, realizing that no one else was at home. I was alone.

I opened the door to a delivery man with a huge bouquet of flowers, strikingly beautiful with lilies and roses. My hands shook as I signed for them. Seeing my distress, he told me he would close the door.

Walking to the kitchen, somehow I knew they were not from my husband, as much as I wanted them to be. Gently, I placed them on the island and opened the card.

"Mom, I am praying for us. I love you always. Brian."

God showed up. Not a minute too soon or a minute too late. In my moment of desperation, He did send help. Back to the bathroom I went, to try to fix my face, but first I fell to the floor. Prostrate. On the face that so desperately needed to be fixed.

"Oh God, I love You! I love You! I love You! You rescued me... thank You!"

Answer me, O Lord, out of the goodness of Your love; in Your great mercy turn to me. Do not hide Your face from Your servant; answer me quickly, for I am in trouble. Come near and rescue me because of my foes. Psalm 69:16-18

Philemon

The pastor just wasn't a great preacher. He usually went "around the world" before he got to any point in his sermons, and then, not much of a point. But he was a man of great compassion and love, just wasn't gifted in that area.

So, I knew.

On this Sunday, when he stated that the Holy Spirit had changed the direction of his message for the day, I knew I should pay attention.

It was in the middle of the previous week when I read these words:

Perhaps the reason he was separated from you for a little while was that you might have him back for good — no longer as a slave, but better than a slave, as a dear brother. He is very dear to me but even dearer to you, both as a man and as a brother in Lord. Philemon 15-16

I sensed when I read it that the Lord was speaking to me, answering the questions of my heart. Why, oh why has this happened? Why is my husband gone? I don't understand. In this one passage, I saw a plan unfold: a plan for his healing and the tenderness of God's heart toward him, and a plan for his return to the Father in just a "little while."

And my heart soared.

When the pastor directed us to open our Bibles to the Book of Philemon, my faith increased as I heard the Lord, for the second time that week, remind me of His plan. Really, who ever preaches on the Book of Philemon? I had never heard a message before or since on that book.

I believe.

For no matter how many promises God has made, they are "Yes" in Christ. 2 Corinthians 3:20

What If? I Will

Let your eyes look straight ahead, fix your gaze directly before you.
Proverbs 4:25

My mind kept wandering.

It was Memorial Day weekend. I was alone. The kids went to spend the weekend with their uncle and aunt in Washington. The questions ran through my mind, "Where was my husband? What was he doing? Who was he with? Will he repent? Will he come home? What if the situation never changes? What if I spend the rest of my days alone?"

God spoke to me: *"What does it matter? I want you to look at Me, look at what I am doing, look at the promises I have made to you, look at your future that I say is good and full of hope. Look at Me, who can do more than you can think or imagine. I am the God of "I will," not the God of "What if?" I will do it. I am doing it. Think on good, pure, right, holy, trustworthy things. I love you."*

What has He promised me? I opened my Bible to the scheduled reading for the day:

"Do not be afraid; you will not suffer shame. Do not fear disgrace; you will not be humiliated. You will forget the shame of your youth and remember no more the reproach of your widowhood. For your Maker is your husband - the Lord Almighty is His name - the Holy One of Israel is your Redeemer; He is called the God of all the earth. The Lord will call you back as if you were a wife deserted and distressed in spirit - a wife who married young, only to be rejected," says your God. *"For a brief moment I abandoned you, but with deep compassion, I will bring you back. In a surge of anger, I hid my face from you for a moment, but with everlasting kindness I will have compassion on you,"* says the Lord your Redeemer. Isaiah 54:4-8

I will not suffer shame.

I will not be humiliated.

I will heal from the abandonment.

I will always have a husband…the Lord Himself.

I will have His deep compassion.

I will have His everlasting kindness.

He is the God of *I will.*

Not the God of *What if?*

Desert Oasis

Desert oasis: an oasis in an isolated area of vegetation in the desert, typically surrounding a spring or similar water source *(wikipedia.org)*

The Lord will guide you always; He will satisfy your needs in a sun-scorched land and will strengthen your frame. You will be like a well-watered garden, like a spring whose waters never fail. Isaiah 58:11

I was in the desert.

A very dry place.

Barren.

As far as I could see into the future...wasteland.

I felt bent over by the weight of it.

Heavy.

But He knows, He sees, He was right there, guiding me.

And even in the desert, His promise is sure. He is my provider.

I didn't remain in the desert.

He guided me out. He made me strong. He carried my burdens. He quenched my thirst.

I am reminded of Jesus' words in the Book of John:

If anyone is thirsty, let him to come to Me and drink. Whoever believes in Me, as the Scripture has said, streams of living water will flow from within him. John 7:37-38

The Living Water will never fail.

He is the oasis in my desert.

The First Thanksgiving

No. Not the Pilgrims and the Indians.

Not that first Thanksgiving.

No. The first Thanksgiving since my husband left our family.

Our three young adult children made their way home for the holiday. Not the twenty or so relatives that we usually hosted. We were still reeling from the pain left in the wake of the abrupt abandonment from my husband.

In the early morning hour, I headed out for my walk and talk with God. I literally wept as I cried out to Him, saying, "Lord, I know I heard from You that You are going after my husband to bring him back to You. But today is Thanksgiving. I cannot bear this. I am starting to lose my confidence."

Returning home, I picked up my Bible and read this:

So do not throw away your confidence; it will be richly rewarded. You need to persevere so that when you have done the will of God, you will receive what He promised. For in just a very little while, He who is coming will come and will not delay. Hebrews 10:35-37

As we shared our Thanksgiving blessings around the table later that afternoon, I recounted God's clear word to me from earlier that morning. Our hearts soared with renewed confidence in Him as He moved our eyes off our pain and back onto His promise.

For the revelation awaits an appointed time; it speaks of the end and will not prove false. Though it linger, wait for it; it will certainly come and will not delay. Habakkuk 2:3

Persevering for the promise…

Radiant

It was finally here...Shannon's wedding day! After months of planning, prepping and planting the yard, for the hundred-plus guests that would gather there to celebrate Shannon and Ryan, it was a beautiful-blue sky, sunny day. Twenty six of the last twenty eight days, it had rained, but on this day, the sun was shining. I had much to do, but took a quick look at my Bible and devotional for the day. I knew I could not get through this day without my God.

Those who look to Him are radiant; their faces are never covered with shame. Psalm 34:5

But shame is what I felt, though.

Deep down in my soul.

Shame that today, on this very special day in my daughter's life, she would be walking down the aisle alone. She could not bring herself to ask her father to do that, it felt hypocritical to her. Shame that though I tried, I could do nothing in my power to bring my husband back to our family. Shame that in the fifteen months since he left, I would have to sit alone in the church, and face many friends and relatives I had not seen during that time. Though there was great joy that my daughter was about to marry the man whom God chose for her, the great sorrow was much too heavy to bear.

Arriving at the church, one of the first people I saw was my dear friend, Kathy. Her words surprised me, "Marti, you look radiant." Shortly thereafter, my sister-in-law, whom I hadn't seen since my husband left, whispered to me, "Marti, you have nothing to be ashamed of."

I remembered His Word.

The day went smoothly with much rejoicing, celebrating this precious union. Then, just like that, it was over. And everyone was gone. My husband was the last to leave. Surely, on this day, God would grab hold of his heart. But it was not so. He wanted to hurry to catch up with the whole group of kids, cousins, aunts and uncles who were gathering at the local pub down the street. He didn't bother to shut the door as he left. I stared at the open door, hoping to see him return through it. I heard the car start in the distance. He was gone again. He wasn't coming back.

The view from the kitchen windows crushed me. The lights still twinkling on the trees, the light gone out in my heart. I cried. I walked around, trying to decide what to do. The silence, the aloneness, was deafening. This isn't the way it was supposed to end.

Within minutes, my son returned. When my husband walked into the pub, my son walked out. Brian walked right through the still open door.

He held me as I cried and he cried. He said, "We don't know why, Mom. We have no answers to the questions. The wedding was great, and you looked radiant today, and Shannon is so happy, and you did awesome, and how wonderful it was that you could give Shannon and Ryan a beautiful wedding. I love you, Mom."

And I cried some more.

As I sobbed in my son's arms, I heard again the words of the Lord from that morning, the rest of the verses…

"Marti sought the Lord, and He answered her; He delivered her from all her fears. Marti looks to Him and is radiant; her face is never covered in shame."

Laying Down

I was in a hurry. I had a routine mammogram scheduled at the Medical Center, then appointments for the rest of the day and into the evening. I quickly read the day's Scripture from the Old Testament. I would read the rest later when I got back. I had been following a plan to read through the Bible in a year, so each day I read from the Old and New Testaments, Psalms and Proverbs.

I will grant peace in the land, and you will lie down and no one will make you afraid. Leviticus 26:6

The mammogram was done as usual, but then the technician asked me to have a seat in the waiting room. That never happened before. She told me she would like to do another test. But just one side. I followed her into an exam room that was down the hall with a different machine.

And back to the waiting room.

The doctor came to get me this time. "Your mammogram shows a mass in your right breast." He said that he would like to check it out with another machine to determine if it was benign. So, I followed him to yet another exam room. He had me lay down on the table, located the mass and after several more scans, told me that is was a benign cyst and nothing needed to be done right now. He advised me to continue to have the yearly mammograms.

It wasn't until later that night, as I sat reading the Word that I saw how very precious His promise was to me that morning. I had laid down on that exam table, and I had not one ounce of fear in me. The technician didn't cause me to be afraid. The doctor didn't cause me to be afraid. The scans and exams didn't cause me to be afraid.

No fear.

Even death had lost its sting. What was there to fear? The very worst that could happen was the very best that could happen. I am so grateful for His good and precious promises. I don't need to be afraid. This life is not all there is…eternity with Jesus awaits.

When the perishable has been clothed with the imperishable, and the mortal with immortality, then the saying that is written will come true: "Death has been swallowed up in victory. Where, O death, is your victory? Where, O death, is your sting?" 1 Corinthians 15:54-55

Taking Jesus at His Word

When Jesus had entered Capernaum, a centurion came to Him, asking for help. "Lord," he said, "my servant lies at home paralyzed and in terrible suffering." Jesus said to him, "I will go and heal him." Matthew 8:5-7

The simplicity of this story strikes me every time I read it. An officer in the Roman army had a problem. One of his servants was at home gravely ill and in terrible pain. When Jesus came into town, the centurion sought His help. He told Jesus about his servant and Jesus simply answered, *I will go and heal him.*

WOW! He asked and Jesus said He would do it. What is Jesus' response to the cry of my heart for help? How does He respond to me and my family that is in "terrible suffering?" Did He tell me that He would heal us? Do we believe Him?

Then Jesus said to the centurion, "Go! It will be done just as you believed it would." And his servant was healed from that very hour. Matthew 8:13

I ask.
Ask and it will be given to you; seek and you will find; knock and the door will be opened to you. For everyone who asks receives; he who seeks finds; and to him who knocks, the door will be opened. Luke 11:9-10

He hears.
Since the first day that you set your mind to gain understanding and to humble yourself before your God, your words were heard. Daniel 10:12

I believe.
Blessed is she who has believed that what the Lord has said to her will be acomplished! Luke 1:45

He heals.
...for I am the Lord, who heals you. Exodus 15:26

Simple, isn't it? Not easy. But simple. I am taking Jesus at His Word.

Promised Land Up Ahead

I was sitting at the computer, working all morning. Hoping, really hoping to finish the book. The eight-year-to-date book that I have been writing.

Wilderness Wanderings…devotions from the desert.

Eight years. Will it ever be finished?

I sensed the Lord say to me recently that it would be finished when He moves me into the Promised Land.

Surely, that's not yet.

I was still desert-dwelling.

So, I took a break. I pondered. I got a glass of water. I went to the bathroom…

…and washing my hands, I noticed the soap. The liquid soap that I bought because it matched the walls in the newly painted room.

Milk and Golden Honey.

I just had to laugh. This God of mine, He sees me, He hears me, He knows me, He speaks to me, He loves me, He was with me…right there in the desert.

The Lord said, "I have indeed seen the misery of My people…I have heard them crying out…and I am concerned about their suffering. So I have come down to rescue them…and to bring them up out of that land into a good and spacious land, a land flowing with milk and honey." Exodus 3:7-8

"Marti, the promised land is coming. I promise. And I keep My promises."

Pause to Ponder

- Is there someone in your life who isn't the person you thought they were? How would your view of them change if you saw them through God's eyes and from His heart?

- Was there a time when God showed up just when you needed Him? Maybe not in the way you wanted or expected, but exactly what you needed.

- God often confirms His promises to us by repetition, when we hear Him speak the same thing multiple times and in various ways. Share about a time when God clearly spoke to you. In what various ways did He speak?

- Name some "what if's" that you are battling. Take a moment to surrender them to God and to focus on and proclaim who God is.

- Share about a time when you were ready to throw in the towel on how God was leading you. What caused you to remain confident in His promise and how did He speak hope into your heart?

- What promises from Scripture do you cling to when facing unknown and potentially fear-inducing situations?

His Peace

The Lord gives strength to His people;
the Lord blesses His people with peace.

Psalm 29:11

Never Shaken

He who does these things will never be shaken, David writes at the end of *Psalm 15.*

It was part of my scheduled Bible reading for the day. Even though I felt pressed for time, I was compelled to look at the verses again.

I needed to find out what was going to keep me unshaken in the midst of the current upheaval in my life. I knew that when God opened the real estate business years before, it was to a higher standard. It was His business. C.U.S.T.O.M. Real Estate. The acronym stands for: Christ with Us in Service To Others is our Mission.

I had to face the realization that the "us" wasn't all of us, and He was being dishonored by some of the agents in the office. My peace was being interrupted. Again.

He who does these things would not be shaken.

- he whose walk is blameless
- he who does what is righteous
- he who speaks the truth from his heart
- he who has no slander on his lips
- he who does his neighbor no wrong
- he who casts no slur on his fellow man
- he who despises a vile man
- he who honors those who fear the Lord
- he who keeps his oath even when it hurts
- he who lends money without usury
- he who does not accept a bribe against the innocent

As I meditated on these verses, slowly God began to emerge a plan of action to maintain the integrity that He established at the beginning. And I was not shaken.

I have set the Lord always before me. Because He is at my right hand, I will not be shaken. Psalm 16:8

Sticks and Stones

"Sticks and stones will break my bones, but words will never hurt me." So goes this nursery rhyme, written in the 1800's.

And so went the conversation with my dear friend, Judy. She shared that this is true for her. She is unaffected by other people's words and opinions. They roll right off of her. As we discussed it further, she attributed it to a great relationship with her dad. She was absolutely secure in him. He not only told her he loved her, but expressed it by his loving actions. Not so with me.

I was still terrified of my father until the day he died. With good reason. And because of that, it was hard to embrace the love of my heavenly Father. I expected judgment, punishment and pain.

As I seek to hear just One Voice, His loving, gentle voice of care and instruction, the other voices are becoming dimmer. Jesus Himself said He did nothing unless the Father told Him to.

So Jesus said, "When you have lifted up the Son of Man, then you will know that I am the one I claim to be and that I do nothing on My own but speak just what the Father has taught Me. The one who sent Me is with Me; He has not left Me alone, for I always do what pleases Him." John 8:28-29

Words can and have hurt me. I am striving to not speak words that hurt others, but rather words of life and encouragement and hope.

Reckless words pierce like a sword, but the tongue of the wise brings healing. Proverbs 12:18

The tongue has the power of life and death. Proverbs 18:21

I want to be more like my friend, Judy, secure in her father's love. I want to be more like Jesus, secure in His Father's love.

There is deceit in the hearts of those who plot evil, but joy for those who promote peace. Proverbs 12:20

Breakfast with the King

He cuts off every branch in me that bears no fruit, while every branch that does bear fruit He prunes so that it will be even more fruitful. John 15:2

I had been walking on the Rails to Trails during my daily early morning time with the Lord. *John 15* had come up recently during a Bible study, and then from a speaker at a meeting the night before.

He had so recently "cut off" a business relationship that had turned abusive toward me. God had to cut it off. I could see that. What I couldn't see was how I was going to survive, since it represented 90 percent of the income that came into the business. I knew it was necessary. Whether cutting or pruning, it is painful.

So, I was walking, praying, and pondering *John 15* when I saw along the side of the trail masses of red raspberries that I hadn't noticed before. I started picking and eating them. The deep, dark red ones were the best, touched with dew and very sweet. I spent a few minutes enjoying these berries when I sensed the Lord speaking to me.

"Marti, I have a plan for you and it's a good plan. You don't need to be afraid. I love you. Now, Marti, how are the berries? Pretty good, huh? Did you go to the store to buy them? Did you need money this morning? Did you have to plant these bushes? Water them? Prune them? Fertilize them? Do you see how much I love you? I am taking care of you today and forever."

Peace flowed over me. Today is all I need to do. I did not need to worry about tomorrow.

I had breakfast with the King.

I have told you these things, so that in Me you may have peace. In this world you will have trouble. But take heart! I have overcome the world. John 16:33

Bulbs

The fear of the Lord is pure, enduring forever. Psalm 19:9

I will fear no evil, for You are with me. Psalm 23:4

There is no doubt that I fear God. But sometimes not in the right way. What fears are rooted deep in me that He wants to expose and heal?

I think of the flower bulbs that I dug up that spring from the grand boys "building site" under the red bud tree, where they used their dump trucks, diggers and shovels. There must have been over one hundred bulbs that I moved to different flower beds in the yard. And yet, right where I thought I had removed them all, some were sprouting.

Three year old Dylan was with me one Saturday, while I dug them up and transplanted them. As I was doing this, I realized Dylan was picking some of them up and throwing them into the creek.

"Oh no, Dylan, Grandma just moved them!"

I went to the water to see the bulbs with fresh growth on them floating down the stream. Is this the picture of the fear in me? Though I have tried to dig it up, I've only moved it around to another spot. Have I transplanted my fear of the future to fear of the present? Is God, like Dylan, wanting to pull it up, root and all, and throw it into the flowing water? So I can watch it float away.

"I hand You the shovel, Lord, so You can dig deep into my heart and pull up the buried roots of fear planted in me at a very early age. Fear of abandonment. Fear of loss. Fear of lacking. Fear of failure. Fear of being alone. Please dig it up and wash it away."

Forever.

Perfect peace drives out fear. 1 John 4:18

For God did not give us a spirit of timidity, but a spirit of power, of love and self-discipline. 2 Timothy 1:7

Checking Out

The last patient of the morning was in the adjusting room, and my mind was already moving through the afternoon cleaning list that needed to be done. Once he was gone, my co-worker would take her break and the bustling office would be quiet.

Shortly, he stepped up to the counter. My checkout greeting varies very little. "All set? That will be $35 for today's visit. Would you like to schedule another appointment?"

I think I said it all without stopping.

He pulled out his wallet and I took the credit card he extended to me. He responded, "No, I will wait and see how I feel...my wife is in your system and you can take her out...she died yesterday...she was diagnosed with cancer eight years ago and for awhile she did well... but then it came back...and we tried lots of treatments...then we went to Mexico and lots of people were getting well there but she didn't...and we came home two weeks ago and I asked her if she wanted to keep fighting and she said no...then she went into hospice..."

I think he said it all without stopping.

Stunned, I barely got in my weak condolences.

His voice trailed off. His shoulders slumped. His sobs were audible. I felt his grief. I felt his loss. I know the loss of a spouse. Not from death. But from abandonment. I know how it feels to have them asleep beside you one day and the next day, the bed is empty.

And the next...and the next...and the next...

Through my own tears and quivering voice, I asked if I could pray for him. My question seemed to startle him. He nodded. I took his hands in mine and did all I knew to do; appeal to the God of heaven and earth to come and surround this dear man with the comfort only He can give. I recalled the suffering Savior who knew grief, a man of sorrows, He who felt as we feel, who promised to send help when we cry out to Him. And I begged that He would do it quickly, in Jesus' name.

He hardly glanced up as he headed to the door. With his hand about ready to push it open, he turned back to look at me and declared:

"I would be one angry man if I didn't know my Lord Jesus Christ."

I sniffled an "Amen."

And declared in my heart:

"I would be one angry woman if I didn't know my Lord Jesus Christ."

Amen and Amen.

Praise be to the God and Father of our Lord Jesus Christ, the Father of compassion and the God of all comfort, who comforts us in our troubles, so that we can comfort those in any trouble with the comfort we ourselves have received from God. 2 Corinthians 1:3-4

Content. Content.

Content: satisfied with what one is or has *(dictionary.com)*

This is what I am learning. Even the Apostle Paul had to learn it. And so it was with me. The dark night of my soul had gone on for far too long, when I cried out to God for that contentment. "Please, teach me to be content!" It didn't happen the way I expected it to happen.

In the past two years, I have laid my head down to sleep in seven different places. Me, who loves my home and feels most "at home" there, is learning to be content wherever God leads me. Learning to rely on Him to meet my needs, satisfied with His provision, confident in His direction of my life.

I am learning...

Paul said: *I know what it is to be in need, and I know what it is to have plenty. I have learned the secret of being content in any and every situation, whether well fed or hungry, whether living in plenty or in want. Philippians 4:12*

Content: everything that is inside of a container, such as the contents of a home *(dictionary.com)*

Because God has moved me to different locations, different jobs and different climates in the last two years, I have found myself leaving behind the contents of my home...except for a suitcase of clothing. So, in the process of learning to be *content,* God has removed much of the *content* from my life.

And that's the secret.

I can live with much less. I can live without what I thought was my security and have found my security in Jesus.

I can do all this through Him who gives me strength. Philippians 4:13

I Lost Hope

Three grand boys were here to help with the Christmas decorations. It was a flurry of activity as they unpacked boxes, asking where each item went. Clay and Reed hung the wreaths on the windows. Dylan strung lights on the star outside and arranged the nativity on the windowsill.

When the flurry ceased, the swag on the staircase was missing its hanging ornament...Hope.

Joy. Peace. Hope.

But now Hope was missing.

It felt fitting. Following the fractured-family feast from the day before, with turkey and stuffing and all the trimmings.

But fatherless. None-the-less.

The soothing sound of my Savior spoke into my spirit.

"My daughter, your Hope isn't missing, just temporarily mis-placed. Your Hope isn't in people or circumstances or things. Your Hope is in Me. And that Hope has not, cannot and will not disappoint. I love you."

Ah, thank You Jesus, my Savior, for saving me again.

And we rejoice in the hope of the glory of God. Not only so, but we also rejoice in our sufferings, because we know that suffering produces perseverance; perseverance, character; and character, hope. And hope does not disappoint us, because God has poured out His love into our hearts by the Holy Spirit, whom He has given us. Romans 5:3-5

Wilderness Walking

When Pharaoh let the people go, God did not lead them on a road through the Philistine country, though that was shorter. For God said, "If they face war, they might change their minds and return to Egypt." Exodus 13:17

I have found myself in the desert of testing and wandering, desperately trying to get out of the wilderness and into the promised land. It's been a really long time in this dry place. I have wondered why God didn't have me take the shorter route, as I have endured grievous suffering and financial destruction.

By day the Lord went ahead of them in the pillar of cloud to guide them on their way and by night a pillar of fire so that they could travel by day or night. Neither the pillar of cloud by day nor the pillar of fire by night left its place in front of the people. Exodus 13:21-22

I have experienced Him right there with me, leading me and lighting the way for the next step He has for me to take. He has proven Himself to me over and over again.

When the dew was gone, thin flakes like frost on the ground appeared on the desert floor. When the Israelites saw it, they said to each other, "What is it?" For they did not know what it was. Moses said to them, "It is the bread the Lord has given you to eat." Exodus 16:14-15

There have been moments on this journey that I have come to realize that God alone is my provider. There were times of such leanness, that if He did not come through, there would not have been enough to eat. I can tell you that He always came through. He cares for His own.

I was young and now I am old, yet I have never seen the righteous forsaken or their children begging bread. Psalm 37:25

Through several outpatient surgeries, an in-patient surgery, and a heart attack scare, Satan has tried to kill, steal and destroy. His plans are to destroy every good thing the Lord has planned for us, including our health. If he can take us out physically, it appears that he has won. But he hasn't. God has proven to be my healer.

But He was pierced for our transgressions, He was crushed for our iniquities; the punishment that brought us peace was upon Him and by His wounds we are healed. Isaiah 53:5

Through many days and many nights of agonizing loneliness, He has become my best friend, my husband and the lover of my soul.

I no longer call you servants because a servant does not know his master's business. Instead, I have called you friends, for everything I learned from My Father, I have made known to you. John 15:15

For your Maker is your husband – the Lord Almighty is His name – the Holy One of Israel is your Redeemer. Isaiah 54:5

I am my lover's and my lover is mine. Song of Songs 6:3

The Lord Himself was walking with me in the wilderness, leading me, loving me, leaving me with the peace that passes all understanding.

On Father's Day...A Letter

To my beloved children: Brian, Lauren and Shannon,

I took a walk this morning on the trail, left around 6:00 a.m.

I have been asking the Lord if I could get a toe ring. You know, it's flip-flop season! Somehow I knew that a toe-ring fell into the category of a want and not a need, so I figured I wouldn't be getting one.

While walking and talking with the Lord, I came upon a sparkly pink, heart-shaped ring. I bent down and picked it up, put it into my pocket and walked on. I wondered if it would fit me.

I did a good amount of work when I got home, finished the mulch that I had left, put the tables away on the porch, watered the flowers, then finally came in and sat down on the couch. I decided to paint my toe-nails and sure enough, when I tried the ring on, it fit!

What I felt this morning was an embrace from my Father. Seems appropriate, doesn't it? Because it is Father's Day. This day won't be as I envisioned it, surrounded by my children, their spouses and my grandkids, celebrating their dad and grandpa, the God-ordained head of our family. And my heavenly Father knows that. So He gave me a gift, a want and not a need. He reminded me that His heart is for me as mine is for Him.

I bless you Brian, my warrior son, whom God has raised up to be a man of integrity and a lover of his family, a Dad to be honored today.

I bless you Lauren and Shannon, women of strength and character, who love, honor and respect their husbands and nurture and cherish their children.

And I pass on to you the everlasting love of our heavenly Father... may His embrace be felt by you today.

God has said, "Never will I leave you; never will I forsake you." Hebrews 13:5

*Though my father and mother forsake me, the Lord will receive me.
Psalm 27:10*

*I am still confident of this: I will see the goodness of the Lord in the land of the living. Wait for the Lord; be strong and take heart and wait for the Lord.
Psalm 27:13-14*

The Full Extent of His Love

It was just before the Passover Feast. Jesus knew that the time had come for Him to leave this world and go to the Father. Having loved His own who were in the world, He now showed them the full extent of His love. John 13:1

This beautiful scene follows those words.

After the meal was over, Jesus got up and took off His coat and wrapped a towel around His waist. He poured water into a basin. Then, He began to wash the disciple's feet. Until He came to Peter, who refused to have Jesus do that for him. He couldn't quite grasp that his Master, his Lord would stoop so low as to wash his feet. Jesus explained that unless He did this for him, Peter would have no part of Him. To which we see Peter's response.

"Then Lord," Simon Peter replied, "not just my feet but my hands and my head as well!" John 13:9

Peter still didn't get it.

Jesus explained that after a person has had a bath, he only needs to have his feet washed because the whole body was already clean. In the context of the times, it was usual for a person to have his feet washed upon entering a home. The streets were not paved and were dusty. The washing of feet was to remove the street dirt, not to get your whole body clean.

Do I get it?

Jesus, my Lord, my King, my Master, went to the cross and died a horrible death, suffering under the weight of the sins of the whole world. My sins. That one act paid the price for sin forever.

That is love.

But it is not the *full* extent of His love.

The *full* extent of His love for me is that He keeps on forgiving me.

He washes my sin away. There is *nothing* that can separate me from His love.

Therefore, since we have been justified through faith, we have peace with God through our Lord Jesus Christ, through whom we have gained access by faith into this grace in which we now stand. Romans 5:1

Pause to Ponder

- What is trying to shake the peace in your life right now? How do the words from *Psalm 15* and *Psalm 16:8* help you?

- Recall a time when you have been hurt by someone's words. Has God healed you of that pain?

- When you have experienced a significant interruption in your life, how did God use that to help you continue to grow in your relationship with Him?

- Is there a deep rooted fear you would like God to replace with His peace? How does this fear hold you back from serving Him more completely?

- Who has God sent into your life to comfort you during a difficult time? Is there anyone that you could pray with to help them feel God's comforting love and peace?

- How do your physical possessions, your "stuff" clutter your life and rob you of peace and joy? How can you be more content?

- What sorts of things have made you feel like you were being thrown into a wilderness of uncertainty and insecurity?

- What kinds of memories does the word "father" bring up? How does this affect the way you relate to God?

His Plans

"For I know the plans I have for you," declares the Lord,
"plans to prosper you and not to harm you,
plans to give you hope and a future."

Jeremiah 29:11

Broken

Shortly after my husband left our family, I flew down to Florida to be with Brian, who was stationed at Hurlburt Field Air Force Base. We had a great need to just be together as we dealt with the excruciating pain. On Sunday morning, we attended a local church. A young Bible school student shared this message.

He spoke of our hearts and how they can get hardened. He had a piece of pottery that he used as an illustration. It was hard, almost brittle. He explained that if he smashed it on the floor, it would break in a multitude of pieces. But if he put it in a dish and poured water over it, in time, it would become soft and pliable again. He went on to say that God wanted our hearts to be soft and He could pour the "Living Water" over us, but sometimes He has to break us, so He can use us.

On the way out of the service, Brian said to me, "Dad needs to be broken." In the pain of the moment, I had to agree.

Several months later, I was reading in Matthew these words of Jesus:

Why do you look at the speck of sawdust in your brother's eye and pay no attention to the plank in your own eye? How can you say to your brother, "Let me take the speck out of your eye," when all the time there is a plank in your own eye? You hypocrite, first take the plank out of your own eye, and then you will see clearly to remove the speck from your brother's eye. Matthew 7:3-5

The illustration of the broken pottery came flooding back into my mind. God spoke to me in that moment:

"It was real easy to see your husband in that pottery, but I wanted you to see you."

I wept with the agony of my failure, my shortcomings, my sin.

And Jesus set me free.

He forgave me because He died for just that reason: my sin.

Have mercy on me, O God, according to Your unfailing love; according to Your great compassion blot out my transgressions. Wash away all my iniquity and cleanse me from my sin. For I know my transgressions, and my sin is always before me. Against You, You only, have I sinned and done what is evil in Your sight. Psalm 51:1-4

Daily, Jesus pours His "Living Water" on me. He and He alone keeps me soft and pliable, so that I will be a useful vessel for Him. So I will be the woman God created me to be.

Jesus answered her, "If you knew the gift of God and who it is that asks you for a drink, you would have asked Him and He would have given you living water." John 4:10

Peter was broken when he heard the rooster crow.

The Lord turned and looked straight at Peter. Then Peter remembered the word the Lord had spoken to him: "Before the rooster crows today, you will disown Me three times." And he went outside and wept bitterly. Luke 22:61-62

David was broken when Nathan told him a story.

Then David said to Nathan, "I have sinned against the Lord." 2 Samuel 12:13

Saul was broken when Jesus appeared to him on the road to Damascus.

As he neared Damascus on his journey, suddenly a light from heaven flashed around him. He fell to the ground and heard a voice say to him, "Saul, Saul, why do you persecute Me?" "Who are You, Lord?" Saul asked. "I am Jesus, whom you are persecuting," He replied. "Now get up and go into the city, and you will be told what you must do." Acts 9:3-6

Jesus was broken when He died for me.

But He was pierced for our transgressions, He was crushed for our iniquities; the punishment that brought us peace was upon Him. Isaiah 53:5

I am broken.

Then the word of the Lord came to me: "O house of Israel, can I not do with you as this potter does?" declares the Lord. "Like clay in the hand of the potter, so are you in My hand, O house of Israel." Jeremiah 18:6

Chocolate-Covered Pretzels

I wasn't supposed to hear it. But I did.

Words spoken by my sister-in-law that hurt.

Not directly to me, but about me.

It was so painful…first I got hurt, and then I wanted to hurt back.

I had all kinds of things go through my mind about what I would say to Cathy, or maybe just send an e-mail to the whole family saying, "Who do you think you are? What right do you have to tell me what to do? Do you even care about me?"

Then I thought maybe I'll just ignore her the next time I saw her… then it turned into maybe I just don't want anything to do with the family ever again…and on…and on…

It was two days later when the Lord finally got a hold of my thought process…it went like this:

"Marti, I love you and you can tell Me all about how you are feeling about Cathy. I love Cathy just like I love you and I want you to love her like that and I was wondering…what rights do you have?"

Well, it was that question that brought me to my knees. I have no rights. I gave them up when I surrendered my life to Jesus. I realized that I had been asking the Lord to give me unconditional love for my extended family and had even prayed that very thing right before I overheard the hurtful comment. I wasn't in the room more than an hour before the Lord tested me.

This is what happened next.

I sensed that I needed to express kindness to Cathy and not what I had been feeling. I went to the cupboard and got out the melting chocolate and pretzels, I had bought a couple of weeks prior, to make chocolate-covered pretzels to send to Brian's family for

Valentine's Day. They were living in South Korea at the time. I found the perfect sized box in the garage, seemingly designed to fit chocolate, pretzels and sprinkles. I wrote a short note, addressed it, and headed to the post office to mail it.

Nick, the postmaster, weighed the box and wanted to know if I needed insurance. He told me it would be $6.50. I told him the contents weren't worth much more than $6.50.

"But is the thought worth $6.50?" he asked.

My answer...an emphatic "Yes!"

For me. I wasn't sure it would mean all that much to Cathy, but I knew the Lord wanted me to do this.

That evening at Bible study, this quote by Elizabeth Elliot was read:

"A cup full of sweetness cannot spill even one drop of bitterness, no matter how jarred."

It was greatly convicting to hear those words and I shared the story of the past few days and how the Lord had brought me to do this act of kindness toward my sister-in-law, because when I was jarred, what came out of me was bitterness. It is not who I want to be. But it is who I am, without the Holy Spirit's control of me. I want to be a sweet, gracious woman who loves others unconditionally...just like Jesus.

Upon receipt of the package, Cathy sent a short e-mail:

Marti,

Thank you so much for the chocolate pretzel supplies. I love chocolate pretzels and I enjoy making them. I will make them next week and send them to the kids for Valentine's Day. I will let you know how they turn out. Thanks for thinking of me. It was sweet.

Cathy

Sweet. A word surely from the Lord Himself. He let me know that indeed I was "jarred" by Cathy's words, but what did come out was "sweet." He did that! What would have come out on my own would have been bitterness.

He made it sweet.

I am ever so grateful.

How sweet are Your words to my taste, sweeter than honey to my mouth! Psalm 119:103

The Teacher

"I am just calling to tell you that I love you," my dear friend Pam said on the other end of the phone. "And I am so thankful for all you are teaching me as you continue in this long, long time of suffering."

"Oh, Pam, I am having a bad day. I don't want to be the teacher," I responded. It was only 7:00 in the morning...did I even have time yet to be "having a bad day?" My answer was real evidence of the weariness and despair that had crept into my being. There just seemed to be no end to the pain...in so many areas of my life. I was facing the finalization of the divorce, the dissolving of the business partnership, the loss of the source of income from the builder I represented, not to mention the physical infirmities. I was at my wits end and I saw no purpose in the pain.

"Do You want me to be the teacher?" I asked the Lord during my morning walk. When I returned home, the story of the woman healed by Jesus, from *Mark 5* was my Bible reading for the day.

A woman who had been very sick, "subject to bleeding" for twelve years, quietly came up behind Jesus and touched the edge of His cloak. In her mind, she said, "If I just touch His clothes, I will be healed." *Immediately,* her bleeding stopped and she felt in her body that she was freed from her suffering. Jesus healed her *immediately*! She had suffered for a very, very long time.

Silently suffered.

Jesus had felt the power go out from Him when the woman touched Him and He turned to the crowd and asked, *"Who touched Me?"* His disciples mentioned the many people gathered around and wondered how He could even ask that question. Jesus waited. Then with fear and trembling, knowing she had been healed, the woman came forward and fell at His feet and told Jesus the "whole truth." This woman had been through so much ridicule and shame. I believe she wanted to just slip away into the crowd.

Sort of like me…

As I read this, I asked myself, "Did Jesus not know the 'whole truth' about this woman?" In other instances in the Bible, it is stated that Jesus knew what people were thinking. Could He not know who touched Him? By her telling her story in front of the large crowd that was gathered, Jesus was glorified. He was seen as the healer. She had tried everything, been to doctor after doctor and spent all she had. Now Jesus healed her. She had an incredible story to tell!

I realized that Jesus wants to do a few things in my life, as well. He wants to "free me from all of my suffering," not just for my relief, but so that others will see Him as the source of that healing. He wants to be "seen" in my life. I could experience His healing and then just slip away into the activities of life, but who would "see" Jesus? Who would know what He can do? Who would know that He is God?

He wants to completely heal me.

He wants to use my pain for His glory.

He wants me to be the teacher.

Daughter, your faith has healed you. Go in peace and be freed from your suffering. Matthew 5:34

Justin

I worked for a short time at the front desk of a local prison ministry. The first thing I noticed about Justin, who was living at the Transition House, was the tattoo of a teardrop in the corner of his right eye. He seemed shy and I had never had a conversation with him, until that day…

He asked Jenna, one of the secretaries, if he could use the phone. She directed him to the one in the room off the hall. When he couldn't get through with the call, he asked her for help. In her usual gruff manner, she punched in a code to override the blocked number. As she walked away, she informed him it was the only time she would do that…just this one time!

When the call didn't go through again, he appeared at the open door of my office. He spoke with desperation in his voice as real tears flowed down over the tattooed teardrop. "Can you help me? I can't ask her again, but I need to call my girlfriend. She is seven months pregnant and she may have to go back to jail today because of…"

I didn't quite understand what he was talking about, but I know what desperation looks like, so I handed him my cell phone to make the call. I could hear some of the conversation and he ended with, "I love you."

He started to walk away and then turned to my desk and said, "Thank you." He was still crying. I asked if he wanted me to pray for him. He said, "Yes!" I took his hands in mine and briefly prayed for him and his girlfriend, asking God for His peace and His protection.

It was later that afternoon when he rushed up to my office, beaming with joy. "It worked, it worked, your prayer worked…she didn't have to go to jail!"

"Praise God!" is what I responded, as he went back out the door. I hadn't prayed that she wouldn't have to go to jail. I just asked for God's peace and His protection. He granted even more than I asked for Justin and his girlfriend.

I never had another conversation with Justin since that day, but every time he saw me, the smile on his face extended from ear to ear. And his tattooed teardrop disappeared into the wrinkles of his eyes.

We didn't need words between us.

The Lord is close to the brokenhearted and saves those who are crushed in spirit. Psalm 34:18

The "Why" Question

The questions would haunt me. The questions to which I have no answer.

"Why doesn't God just bring your husband home?"

"Why would God allow so much suffering in your family?"

"Why did this happen to you?"

I was reading in the gospel of John one day about a man who was born blind. The disciples had a question for Jesus. They wanted to know why this man was born blind. And they had a few of their own theories as to why. He must have sinned, or maybe his parents sinned. There had to be a reason why this happened to him.

Jesus had an answer. *This happened so that the work of God might be displayed in his life. John 9:3*

Then Jesus proceeded to heal the blind man. Rather unconventionally, I might add. Of course, an explainable miracle is probably not a miracle. Jesus mixed His saliva and dirt to make mud, put it on the man's eyes and sent him to wash off in the Pool of Siloam. He obeyed and it states that he came home seeing.

Miraculously healed.

This man told his story over and over again.

There are still so many questions I cannot answer. I have come to realize that I don't need to answer them. There are lots of reasons why bad things happen. God has not called me to understand, but rather to trust Him.

The answer to the "Why?" question for me has become...so God's work will be seen in my life. God is healing me to tell His stories over and over again, so He gets the glory.

They will tell of the power of Your awesome works, and I will proclaim Your great deeds. Psalm 145:6

A Gaggle of Grands

I have nine living, breathing, marvelous, spunky, fun, grandchildren.

And one in heaven.

My daughter, Shannon, is a professional photographer. Over the years, she has taken lots of pictures of these little ones, that aren't so little anymore. They came fast and furiously.

All three of my children were married within nine months. Then came a boy, a boy, a boy, a boy, a boy, a boy. Six grand boys in three and a half years! Oh my, was I never going to get to buy something *pink?* Oh, yes, I would…after each couple had their two boys, they each had a girl.

But, through all these years and all these photos, I never once had a professional photo taken with all of the grandchildren. It just didn't seem right. It seemed that their grandfather should be in the photo.

Brian and Amanda had been out of the area for a number of years and finally moved closer to us, to the Washington, D.C. area. We could actually drive to see them, and not have to take a plane.

It was that first summer, when we were *all* together, that I asked Shannon if she would take a photo for me with my grandkids. I do what grandmas do. I bought matching outfits. I was able to get great deals at the local outlets on shirts for the boys and dresses for the little girls. The photo session wasn't easy, but Shannon was able to capture a beautiful photo of us. Later that summer, my kids gave me a large canvas print of it that hangs in my hallway. It also travels with me. As God has led me and opened doors to tell of His amazing grace in my life at women's events, it has become the centerpiece of my story.

I display this treasured picture at the end as I conclude that my life, my purpose, my desire is to bring glory to God and to tell of His wonderful works.

We will not hide them from their children; we will tell the next generation the praiseworthy deeds of the Lord, His power and the wonders He has done. Psalm 78:4

This gaggle of grands is the next generation.

A Fool or a Follower

The fire pit was full of smoldering ash.

It was time to clean out the house. My daughter, Lauren, said I had a lot of stuff. She and Chris were interested in buying the house that my ex-husband and I had built for our retirement.

Going through all the papers from the vacation property in the mountains we had owned, all the papers threatening divorce, then the divorce itself, the papers from the business I owned and had to close. All of it made me ill.

Destruction. All over the place. It took several days to burn it all. And now I was looking at the ash heap of my life.

"I need a break, Lord. A giant God-sized break."

My dreams. Dead.

Hope to be husband and wife again. Dead.

Financial security. Dead.

Years and years of hoping for my husband to come home, only to realize that my whole marriage was a lie. My husband spent all of them longing for a life he didn't get to have.

And I felt like a fool.

Jim Elliot, missionary to the Quechua Indians, wrote in his journal before being killed by them, "He is no fool who gives what he cannot keep to gain that which he cannot lose." *

What is it that I have given up? My comfort. My desires. That longing to be held, talked to, treated well and with respect and kindness, spoken to with a gentle tongue. I have given up the very fulfillment of the needs You gave me. They remain unmet. For years. And more years just stretch on in front of me. No end in sight. What am I gaining that cannot be lost? Obedience to God. You said to walk this hard path. And I said, "Yes." Believing with all I am that the very hard path would lead to unspeakable joy.

I have lost that hope. I don't know how to restore that hope. Or if God even wants me to. Maybe He has the hope dying, not me. Maybe even that mustard seed of hope has to die in order for Him to bring new life.

There is nothing to restore. Perhaps there never was. And that realization just burns through my veins. Like the smoldering ash heap.

Fool. Fool. You are a fool. You gave your very life, your heart, your soul and your body to a man who would not or perhaps just could not love you back.

A fool. Just like Jim Elliot, who laid down his life for the Quechua Indians of Ecuador to know Jesus. And they killed him.

Just like I feel right now. Dead. At the hands of the one I loved.

The Quechua Indians did come to know Jesus, after they took Jim Elliot's life. It cost him everything. But he gained everything. And heaven is for real. And the Quechua Indians are valuable to God and sometimes He requires a big price to be paid.

I am no fool.

I am His follower.

This is how we know what love is: Jesus Christ laid down His life for us. And we ought to lay down our lives for our brothers. 1 John 3:16

* *In The Shadow of the Almighty* by Elizabeth Elliot

Zip-lining

I was walking up the hill from my room to the retreat center, preparing my heart to tell my story publically for the first time, when I heard a still, small voice, *"Your life is like a zip line. Use that analogy."*

And so I did. It made perfect sense in the telling of my story, as I moved forward and backwards again to fill in the details that needed to be clarified. And it freed the women listening from trying to figure it all out chronologically. And it's just so true...

My life is like a zip-line. And the older I get, the faster it goes. I am zipping along to that finish line, where I long to hear these words from Jesus: *Well done, good and faithful servant! Matthew 25:21*

Fast forward on that zip-line a little over a year later. I had spoken again at the same facility, where my dear friend attended. After the event, Heidi asked a simple question:

"Have you ever zip-lined?"

"Uh, no, but it's a great analogy."

"Not great if you've never done it."

Oh, dear. I knew I was in trouble. By the next day, she had secured passes to a local zip-line course.

On a sunny autumn day, the trees bursting in golds, rusts and crimson, we climbed up to that first shaky platform. Of seven. Rising to over seven stories high. We had an excellent guide, encouraging, patient, funny. It felt like forever until I got the courage to take a step. He waited. He stated:

"Just one step off the platform, then you'll soar."

Seven times I took just that one step. Seven times I soared.

I can't tell you that now I love zip-lining. Adventures for me have my feet closer to the ground. But I will tell you that I am glad I did it. I never got unafraid to take just one step off that platform. And, so far, I have never been unafraid to take just one step up to the platform to tell my story. But one step I must take. For when I tell my story, He gets the glory and others get the courage to tell theirs. The Spirit comes to heal and set His people free.

And they soar.

Even youths grow tired and weary, and young men stumble and fall; but those who hope in the Lord will renew their strength. They will soar on wings like eagles; they will run and not grow weary, they will walk and not be faint. Isaiah 40:30-31

My life is like a zip-line. The older I get, the faster it goes. I am zipping along to that finish line, where I long to hear these words from Jesus:

Well done, good and faithful servant! Matthew 25:21

Love Struck

As we were floating across the Sea of Galilee, the overwhelming reality struck me that I was here, actually here, in Israel, against all odds, in the land where Jesus walked. The dark lenses of my sunglasses covered my red rimmed eyes as the tears of gratitude spilled down my cheeks.

I looked toward the shoreline and even more emotion overtook me. I desired for a long time to be in Israel where Jesus had walked and here I was gliding over the waters of the lake where He actually walked, as recorded in the gospels of Matthew, Mark and John.

During the fourth watch of the night Jesus went out to them, walking on the lake. Matthew 14:25.

As we arrived on the shore and exited the boat, I turned to the gentleman behind me and said, "I just love Jesus more today than yesterday."

He grinned.

Love-struck: having a passionate or overwhelming feeling of love, smitten *(dictionary.com)*

What a gift it was to visit the land of Israel, so rich in history, so significant to my faith. Not only did I meet my God there, I met His people. When the Spirit in me meets the Spirit in others - joy jumps, hope happens, intimacy is.

The very reason we are alive is to love Him, because He first loved us.

Love the Lord your God with all your heart and with all your soul and with all your strength. Deuteronomy 6:5

Inked

"Is that a tattoo? Why did you do that?" was the shocked question from my older brother, while we chatted at a family get-together.

"Because I wanted to," was my confident reply. It felt good to say I did something, perceivably "out of character," just because I had a desire to do it.

I went on to explain that the tattooed word *Yeshua* means "Jesus" in Hebrew. Having been to Israel at the beginning of that year changed me, in ways I am still discovering. I met Jesus there in so many tangible ways, and He is rapidly unfolding His plans for me to serve Him the rest of my days.

"Well, when did you do it? Did it hurt? You're the only one in our family that has a tattoo!"

Interestingly, it wasn't planned for that day on purpose. But I had it done on July 1st, which was the first day of the second half of the year that He said would be *new* and *now*. It stung a little but was finished in about fifteen minutes. And it really didn't matter if I was the "only one" that had a tattoo. For me, it represented being linked to Jesus forever.

Or inked.

We are intimately linked in this harvest work. Anyone who accepts what you do accepts Me, the One who sent you. Anyone who accepts what I do accepts My Father, who sent Me. Accepting a messenger of God is as good as being God's messenger. Accepting someone's help is as good as giving someone help. This is a large work I've called you into, but don't be overwhelmed by it. It's best to start small. Give a cup of cool water to someone who is thirsty, for instance. The smallest act of giving or receiving makes you a true apprentice. You won't lose out on a thing. Matthew 10:40 (The Message Bible)

Pause to Ponder

- Has God ever "broken" you so He can use you? Describe how you were broken and how He used you as a result of being broken.

- How do you typically respond to "hurtful" words? Describe some practical ways you can turn bitter feelings into sweet ones.

- Have you experienced a season of silent suffering, weariness or despair? Have you been freed from this suffering and experienced purpose in your pain?

- Describe a time when you have lost hope. Is your hope still lost? How can lost hope be restored?

- Tell about a time when you have taken a fearful or courageous step forward. Did you soar?

- Describe a time when God answered a specific prayer.

- Has God ever clearly answered a "why" question you had? If so, describe how your question was answered. If not, what is He teaching you as you wait for His answer?

His Promised Land

It surely wasn't planned.

Just a few days before what would have been the end of my 40th year of marriage, I finished this book. The timing represents to me that my "wilderness wanderings" are over. The "promised land" that I was expecting isn't the one that I am experiencing. The one I anticipated was a marriage restored, with both of us serving God together and enjoying our latter years in our own paradise.

Paradise isn't for now.

Paradise is where we'll spend all of eternity, worshipping the One who is worthy to receive all glory, honor and praise.

Paradise, where there will be no more suffering, no more tears, no more pain.

Paradise, where the streets are gold and there is no sun and there is no moon, for the Lamb of God will be its Light.

No. God has not brought me into paradise. God has not brought me into my own "promised land." But He has led me into His Promised Land.

The Promised Land, where there are still giants to be defeated, but He fights the battles for me.

The Promised Land, where there is still loneliness, but He has become my ever present companion.

The Promised Land, where there are still storms that rage, but He calms every one.

I live in His Presence.

I have His Provision.

I am covered with His Protection.

I experience His Power.

I trust in His Promises.

I rest in His Peace.

I know His Plans for me are good.

The wilderness wanderings are over…He has brought me into His Promised Land.

The Lord your God has blessed you in all the work of your hands. He has watched over your journey through this vast desert. These forty years, the Lord your God has been with you, and you have not lacked anything.
Deuteronomy 2:7

About the Author

Marti Evans resides in south central Pennsylvania. She is the mother of three grown children and grandmother to nine energetic youngsters.

For many years she has taken a walk with Jesus every day, seeking to separate herself for Him, striving to hear only His voice, and receive direction for every step she takes.

Marti is the founder of One Step Ministries and is available to share the story of God's amazing grace in her life and the redemptive power of the Holy Spirit that He desires for everyone.

Marti can be reached at:
One Step Ministries
martievans.org
onestepministries@martievans.org
facebook.com/marti.evans
717-269-0442

What is impossible with man is possible with God.

Luke 18:27